The Men ~~Who~~ ~~Changed~~ the Course of American History

Washington, Franklin, Hamilton, Lincoln, M.L. King, Reagan, & Roosevelt. Lessons from the Great Men that Forged the United States of America.

- SECOND EDITION -

By Dominique Atkinson

DISCLAIMER

The information provided herein is stated to be truthful and consistent, in that any liability, in terms of inattention or otherwise, by any usage or abusage of any policies, processes, or directions contained within is the solitary and utter responsibility of the recipient reader. Under no circumstances will any legal responsibility or blame be held against the publisher for any reparation, damages, or monetary loss due to the information herein, either directly or indirectly. Respective authors hold all rights not held by publisher.

Author's Note

These American men who changed the course of history are remarkable not merely for their accomplishments, but because they were born in ordinary circumstances and rose to prominence thanks to their resourcefulness, personalities, and convictions. The world knows who they are by name and by reputation, yet at their births, it's doubtful that even doting parents expected them to rise to the levels of prominence which they achieved.

Had they been born in modern times, they would have been served by an entourage of press agents and publicists to promote their achievements. But only Ronald Reagan, who served as president of the United States from 1980-1988, lived in a time when self-promotion was expected, and the strength of his appeal resided in his ability to conjure an idyllic image from American mythology, when small-town values and virtues would triumph over sophisticated city cynicism. Benjamin Franklin charmed the notoriously selective French with his shrewd rendition of what they assumed was a typical American, combined with his genuine fondness for the ladies. Alexander

Hamilton wheeled and dealed for that most middle class of virtues: the necessity to pay bills in order to demonstrate financial credibility. The Roosevelt cousins, Theodore and Franklin, were raised in privilege but made the common man a cornerstone of their presidencies. Abraham Lincoln's frontier wit and storytelling did not make him the darling of Washington's drawing rooms, but it connected him to the people and helped him survive the emotional demands of his office at a time when he was often at odds with his generals, his Cabinet, the press and even his wife. Martin Luther King, Jr.'s soaring oratory lent his campaign for civil rights a poetic glory that stirred his followers at a time of enormous suffering and upheaval for African-Americans, whose simple quest was to be treated as equals. And what is there to say about George Washington that has not already been said? Would the United States have flourished as it has without him at the helm for the nation's introduction into independence? He was not born to the nobility or even to the landed gentry of his home colony of Virginia. His characteristic self-control, integrity, and attention to duty would have earned the scorn of the British aristocracy who wielded power in the nation from which the colonies sought independence, and yet those traits triumphed over the British, who ruled by pedigree rather than ability.

Join me in learning about these great men! It's by studying their lives that we gain a sense, not only of who they were, but of what we have become as a country because of their influence. If any of these men were to be taken out of history's record, the ensuing gap would be enormous. As we study the past, we can look back on their achievements and be glad that we journey upon the roads that they paved for history to travel.

The United States of America is built upon the foundation that these men created. Without them, the nation, had it even survived its political infancy, would not be the dynamic, thriving power it is today.

TABLE OF CONTENTS

Chapter 1 - George Washington: The Father of His Country

Who was George Washington?

Upon learning that the man who had beaten his mighty army planned to resign his commission at the end of the war and return home to his private life, Great Britain's King George III said, "If he does that, he will be the greatest man in the world." High praise indeed, from a monarch referring to the common-born colonial who had led the American military war for independence against the British. Washington did just that; resigning as commander of the army so that he could return home to Mount Vernon, Virginia and, he hoped, the life of a planter. King George may have suffered from episodes of insanity caused by the disease porphyria, but in this incident of lucidity, he proved to be quite perceptive. But the world did not understand the tall, imposing Virginian who would respond, whenever he was called upon, to serve his country when needed. It was not power that Washington craved: it was honor. Throughout his life, he sought to maintain his dignity as much as he maintained his rank.

The man who was known, in his own lifetime, as the Father of His Country, was a man who put duty above pleasure. He was steadfast, self-disciplined, tall and commanding in appearance, and focused in pursuit of his goals. He was also hot-tempered and not without vanity; when he was called to Philadelphia by the Continental Congress, he stopped first at his tailor, so that a uniform that he had designed could be made for him to wear. He led his troops both by personal example and by strong military discipline, but he managed to inspire their loyalty through the long years of conflict. He returned to the national stage after the war to preside over the convention charged with writing the Constitution of the United States and, when that hallowed document was created, he stayed to become the fledgling nation's first president. His driving desire was to be at his home, but when his nation needed him, he put his personal goals aside and did his duty.

He is regarded by many as the best of all the 44 presidents, and certainly among those few who are regarded as the very best. His likeness is preserved upon Mount Rushmore, it's seen daily in transactions with the dollar bill and the quarter. Sometimes, that's where our knowledge of the first president ends: an image, stern and unyielding and unemotional. Who was the real Washington, the man who loved to dance, who made provisions in his will to free his slaves, who treated young officers such as the Marquis de Lafayette like the sons he never had? We know the military commander, the political leader and the president, but who was George Washington, the man?

In the Beginning

Born in Virginia in 1731, George Washington had an older brother, Lawrence, who was the heir to the family estate. The Washingtons didn't belong to Virginian's elite, but they were prosperous tobacco farmers who, like their successful neighbors, owned slaves who performed the physical labor upon which the South's economy depended. Augustine Washington sent his older sons Lawrence and Augustine to be educated in England. But Washington's father died when Washington was 11, leaving his older half-brother Lawrence in charge and the boy to receive his education from tutors. It was Lawrence Washington who first owned the Potomac River plantation that he named Mount Vernon in honor of his commanding officer.

The elder Washington used his connections with his influential in-laws, the Fairfaxes, to get his half-brother a position at the age of 17 as official surveyor for Culpeper County, Virginia. This not only launched George Washington into a successful and well-paying career, but also made it possible for him to begin acquiring land, that readily available commodity in an untamed wilderness that could raise a man's social status. Fortunately, land provided an ample source of currency for young men of initiative and his rise in status would help him gain a wealthy widow when it was time to wed.

Brother Lawrence's connections also brought Washington to the attention of The Ohio Company, a land investment company, and the Virginia militia. But even an ambitious young man like Washington respected his obligations to his family, concerns which would always play an important role in his life. In 1751, he accompanied his brother, who was suffering from tuberculosis, to Barbados in the hopes that the climate would cure his disease. Unfortunately, tuberculous was one of numerous deadly maladies of that time, and Lawrence Washington died at home a year later, leaving his land to his half-brother, George Washington.

Washington Gets Noticed

Virginia was a settled colony and perhaps the most powerful and influential of the 13, but westward expansion was constantly in motion and the Ohio Company's British investors were eager to claim the land stretching ahead. So were the French, as the two longtime European enemies continued their rivalry on the soil of the American continent. Both sides wanted to control the Ohio Valley. However, the diplomatic practices of the European courts had been transplanted to the rugged New World. In 1753, Virginia Colony's Lieutenant Governor Robert Dinwiddie sent Washington with a letter to the French to ask them to leave the Ohio Valley. It was an opportunity that an ambitious 22-year old was eager to accept. As might have been expected, the French commander refused to leave. The venture was not a success in military terms, but nonetheless, Washington was making a name for himself, and he was given a commission to raise a company of 100 men.

When he was sent by Dinwiddie to guard the building of a fort in what is present-day Pittsburgh, Pennsylvania, a battle with the French ensued. The battle lasted approximately 15 minutes, but the notoriety would linger throughout Washington's early career. The French commander Joseph Coulon de

14

Jumonville was killed, possibly by Washington's Indian allies. The French rallied and captured Washington at Fort Necessity. Washington's education had not provided him with the courtier's linguistic introduction to French, the Western language of diplomacy; he signed the surrender, not realizing that in doing so, he confessed that Jumonville had been assassinated. The episode, although thousands of miles away from the proximity of conflict which dominated European's landscape, was an international one. Washington cannot be blamed for setting off the Seven Years War between France and England, more commonly known as the French and Indian War, but his actions played a part. The stakes were high when the ultimate prize was a continent of rich natural resources, and a bloody conflict ensued.

Washington was made a colonel of a Virginia regiment charged with defending the colony's frontier. Rigorous training instilled military discipline in his men; numerous battles made them and their leader experienced. He admired the discipline of the professional army as opposed to the unreliable militia soldiers. The British ended up the victors in the war and Washington had honed his military skills by working with them. He had paid attention to the lessons and he recognized that soldiering was not a game for amateurs. No one could have guessed that the next time he put those skills to use, it would be against his former mentors.

Back home at Mount Vernon, Washington turned his attentions to domestic life. In 1759, he married the wealthy widow Martha Dandridge Custis, becoming stepfather to her young son and daughter. Upon becoming a husband, Washington was suddenly a wealthy man, in fact, one of the wealthiest in Virginia. But he was also buying land on his own and increasing his holdings, including slaves. He lived the life of the planter gentry, became a member of the House of Burgesses, hunted, danced, went to parties, and played cards. But unlike most planters, who lived their lives owing money, he was practicing sound financial practices which would get him out of debt by switching his main crop from tobacco to wheat, as well as milling flour, fishing, breeding horses, and producing whiskey. By Virginia standards, he had achieved the heights of success.

Washington the Husband

By anyone's standards, George Washington made a good marriage when he wedded the wealthy widow Martha Dandridge Custis in 1759. It's highly unlikely that either of the partners could have predicted the direction their lives would take as their position as landed gentry of Virginia would take on national status in time. She may have fancied military men; her first husband was Colonel Daniel Parke Custis. She was 19 when she married Custis; they had four children who were born from 1751-1757. Two of the children died young, and when her husband died unexpectedly in 1757, Martha Custis was a 26-year old widow with two small children to raise. But she was a wealthy widow who owned over 17,000 acres of land and almost 300 slaves. Widowhood gave her an economic independence she couldn't claim as a wife; because Custis died without a will, she was the executor of the estate and possessed the right to buy and sell property and make contracts. Because of her financial wealth, she could remarry if and when she chose; she would not have to do so for money. Widows did not remain unmarried for long at that time, and from all accounts, the Custis marriage was a happy one.

But she was not destined to remain a widow. When Washington was in Williamsburg in 1758, he likely learned about the attractive young widow. He visited her at her home; he wrote in his account book that he had left generous tips for her household slaves, perhaps hoping to make a good impression on the people who served her. Within months, Washington was making improvements to Mount Vernon and the widow Custis was ordering clothes from London that included wedding garments and purple slippers. They must have made an interesting couple: Washington was an imposing and towering six feet, two inches tall; Martha a diminutive five feet. But the couple must have liked what they saw in one another. Martha, who could have followed the example of other colonial widows who opted for the equivalent of a "prenup" did not have her new husband sign a binding premarital contract that would have protected her assets. Washington not only had the use of "the widow's third" for as long as she lived, but he was also the legal guardian of her children, in charge of overseeing and protecting their financial affairs.

In 1759, ten months after their first meeting, she and George Washington were married; she and her children Jacky and Patsy moved to Mount Vernon, which was a 2000-acre estate located in Northern Virginia along the banks of the Potomac. The home that Washington inherited from his brother's widow would be their home, but Martha traveled where her husband went. Like her husband, she recognized her duty, and although she cherished life at home at Mt. Vernon, she recognized that she was not married to a man who would live in the shadows.

Washington Takes the Stage

Washington was not at heart a revolutionary, but he was a man of business, and he took exception to the imposition of taxes by England. Southerners imported a great many luxury goods from Europe, and with those goods came taxes. He supported the boycott of English goods until the Townsend Acts were repealed. In 1774 he was chosen as a delegate to the First Continental Congress. By 1775, the colonies were at war against Great Britain, and Washington was chosen as commander of the Continental Army. It must have seemed an audacious act to the British for this untried company and this untitled colonial to think that they could mount a military campaign against the battle-hardened, experienced British army. The British military leadership had little respect for their American counterparts, or for the raw country which bred these upstarts.

The Continental Congress was unused to leading, but Washington suffered from no such inhibition. Washington was not often victorious in battle, but he never surrendered his army and as long as he had soldiers, the war was winnable. His tactics frustrated the British, who expected to defeat their enemies as they had successfully done throughout their history. The colonial army attracted foreign officers like Baron von Steuben and the Marquis de Lafayette, and as the war continued, its American leaders began to prove their merit. But the war was arduous. The Americans didn't have enough gunpowder or weapons, there were times, particularly at Valley Forge, when they didn't even have shoes, and they were disparaged by their foes.

But they had Washington: tall, unflappable, resolute, courageous, who won when he had to, survived the treason of Benedict Arnold, and endured the relentless winters and privation. Armies didn't fight during the winter, and so Washington asked his wife to join him at the army's military encampment. Before she made the first journey to the army's winter quarters, she had to be inoculated for smallpox, a deadly disease at that time, particularly among soldiers. During the terrible winter at Valley Forge, Martha Washington shared her husband's winter quarters, as well as staying with him during military campaigns in New Jersey, New York, Maryland, and Pennsylvania. She became friends with the wives of the other generals who joined their husbands, included Lucy Knox and Kitty Greene, the wives of Henry Knox and Nathaniel Green. The wealthy Virginian did not lead a life of leisure during these months, as she received visitors, acted as her husband's secretary, visited the soldiers who were sick and wounded, and coordinated activities that livened the season and created a social center in the camp.

When winter ended, the armies returned to their martial purpose of engaging in battle. When the French government was inspired by the victory at Saratoga to join the Americans against the British, the tide of battle turned to favor the colonials, and in 1781, the French and American troops witnessed the surrender of Great Britain to her former colonies. His duty done, Washington went home. He did not overthrow the government, he did not seek to become monarch. In his decorum, he confounded the Old World which was unacquainted with this novel sense of honor.

He had the opportunity to turn his military leadership into political control. Soldiers after the war were angered over the failure of Congress to award them promised back pay. The officers began to circulate an anonymous letter supporting a revolt against Congress which had failed to recognize its obligations to its veterans. Washington heard of the events and issued an order that forbade unauthorized meetings. He met with the officers and advised them to do nothing which would sully their achievements as soldiers in the victorious war against Britain. When he reached in his pocket for a letter from a member of the Continental Congress, he took out a pair of spectacles. He apologized for his poor vision, saying, "Gentlemen, you must pardon me. I have grown old in the service of my company and now find that I am growing blind." His efforts were successful; the threatened rebellion dissolved.

The war for independence was won, but the fight to govern had only just begun. Four years after he returned to Mount Vernon, Washington was asked to be a delegate to the Constitutional Convention in Philadelphia. He was unanimously elected its president. Having seen how a weak central government had made his role as military leader difficult, Washington supported ratification of the Constitution because he felt that the alternative was anarchy. From being the president of the Convention, Washington became the president of the United States, the country's first president. There was no other candidate, and no one could imagine anyone else in the position. Upon taking the brief oath of office and promising to preserve, protect and defend the Constitution, Washington added the phrase "so help me God," a concluding phrase which many, although not all, of his successors have uttered as they in turn, followed in his path.

It was significant that the man in America who had, throughout his career, commanded more influence than any other American, was mindful of the need not to seek it. When he arrived in the Capitol city before the members of Congress, newly elected, showed up, Washington waited for Congress to convene instead of taking the opportunity to seize power

Washington served two terms as president. They were eventful; the United States was an untried player in the world of governance. Washington had a keen sense of his place in history, and in the days before his inauguration, he often commented that he was walking on untrodden ground. He was aware that the trust placed in him by his countrymen was also a challenge: to him fell the task of defining the executive band of the government without turning into a tyrant or adopting the habits of a monarch.

What should a president be called? Suggestions included "His Excellency" and "His Highness" but Washington suggested "Mr. President" which has a less imperial, more egalitarian tone. The suit he wore as his first inauguration was simple brown broadcloth, with nothing of the majestic to set him apart from the others.

It was Washington who appointed advisors, known as the Cabinet, who would oversee major areas of governance. His original Cabinet held four posts: Secretary of State Thomas Jefferson; Secretary of the Treasury Alexander Hamilton; Secretary of War Henry Knox; and Attorney General Edmund Randolph. Washington chose with an eye for both ability and geography; Jefferson and Randolph were Virginians like Washington; Alexander Hamilton was originally from the West Indies but had settled in New York; and Henry Knox, a Bostonian.

Martha Washington also had to travel upon untrodden ground in her role as what would become known, although not during her tenure, as the First Lady. She was usually referred to as Lady Washington, although some called her "Lady Presidentess." Daily she received visitors and made calls upon New York City's (the temporary capital) important members of society. She hosted weekly receptions on Friday evenings where members of Congress, dignitaries, and local residents of prominence attended, enjoyed refreshments, and visited with one another after being presented to the president's wife. She was an experienced hostess and household manager, but she admitted to her niece that her role as the president's wife made her feel like a state prisoner.

During his terms, Washington supported Secretary of the Treasury Hamilton's actions to make the country financially sound. The nation's capital was established on the Potomac River; it would eventually be named Washington City in his honor after he was no longer in office. When frontiersmen protested the government's tax on distilled spirits, Washington sent in state militias, with himself in command, to put down the rebellion, the only time that a sitting American president has led troops into battle. His terms of office ended, once more Washington returned home to Mount Vernon where he could focus on his role as a planter.

Washington was a man of dedication to his duty and nothing, not even inclement weather, could interfere with his commitment to a task. On a snowy day in December, 1799, Washington, maintaining the daily schedule of riding his lands to inspect his plantation, became ill. He died on December 14. In his will, he freed his valet, William Lee, who had been at his side throughout the war. His other slaves were to be freed upon his wife's death; however, Martha freed them a year after he died. Washington, in whose life there was so much military turmoil and political tumult, died in peace. His final words were "'Tis well."

Why Was Washington Important?

Washington's crucial role in the birth of the nation can't be emphasized enough. By abstaining from the trappings of power, he served as a model for future presidents in how to manage the office to which they were elected. He limited himself to two terms, a practice which was only broken by Franklin Delano Roosevelt, but the two-term presidency subsequently became the law of the land when the 22nd amendment was added to the Constitution. He kept a steady hand at the tiller of the nation's direction, avoiding foreign entanglements, encouraging trade and sound commerce, establishing a form of leadership in which substance superseded style. Henry Lee, a military colleague of Washington and a fellow Virginian, said it best when he described Washington as "first in war, first in peace, and first in the hearts of his countrymen."

The United States might have turned out very differently had someone other than George Washington first occupied the presidency. For Washington, doing the right thing was paramount. He was mindful of his image and his reputation, but he was not enslaved by acclamation. He wrote, "Though I prize as I ought the good opinion of my fellow citizens, yet, if I know myself, I would not seek or retain popularity at the expense of one social duty or moral virtue."

He was not flamboyant or a man of cutting-edge ideas. He believed fervently in doing his duty as a Virginian, as a planter, as a husband and stepfather, as a general, a delegate, a president. He was no ideologue but even as a pragmatist, he recognized that the United States would have to come to a decision on the issue of slavery. For Washington, it was sufficient to free them in his will, but the nation would grapple with the matter to the point of bloodshed. Of this, Washington said to an acquaintance, "I can foresee that nothing but the rooting out of slavery can perpetuate the existence of our union."

It can be said with some conviction that George Washington invented the office of the president. Because Congress respected his authority so completely, his choice of advisors to serve in his Cabinet was not challenged, giving future presidents the right to choose for themselves who would serve in those roles. By selecting the Supreme Court Chief Justice, Washington replaced him without regard to seniority, providing future presidents with the ability to seek candidates beyond the immediate candidates.

He invented executive privilege when he refused to deliver records related to the Jay Treaty of 1795 to the House of Representatives. Yet he recognized the boundaries that separated the branches of government and did not try to influence the legislative or judicial branches when he sponsored the proposals submitted to Congress. He made no attempt to profit from his presidency or promote friendships with his influence and power. His hope that the country would not divide into political parties was doomed to disappointment, but his successors were not Washington, and they saw the presidency as part of their career path. For Washington, serving as president was answering the country's call, as he had done whenever he was needed.

Chapter 2 - Alexander Hamilton: America's Moneyman

Who was Alexander Hamilton?

Alexander Hamilton always had an eye for the ladies, so possibly he might have recognized the irony that will see his face replaced on the currency with the image of a prominent woman in American history. For the time being, Alexander Hamilton is the face on the ten-dollar bill, indicating that there was a time when he stood among the ranks of his fellow Founding Fathers. What's forgotten is that he was acknowledged to be the equal in talent and ability to Washington, Jefferson, Adams, Franklin and the other Founding Fathers whose names are better known. Long before the character known as Deep Throat advised Watergate reporters Woodward and Bernstein to "follow the money," Hamilton was leading the post-war, debt-ridden United States along a path that would establish the nation's financial solvency. Perhaps he, more than any of the others, deserves to be commemorated on the nation's currency.

The first secretary of the treasury, appointed by George Washington who had a strong bond with the clever, capable man who had formerly been his aide-de-camp during the Revolutionary War, Hamilton was a self-educated man with an instinct for finance. The illegitimate result of an adulterous liaison between his married mother and a Scottish merchant, Hamilton, who was described by John Adams as "the bastard brat of a Scottish peddler" may have lacked a proper entry into the world, but he proved himself capable of making his own way with his own skills, frequently on his own terms.

Alexander Hamilton was present when the new nation was being midwifed from a sprawling collection of colonies into a cohesive union of states. He was a favorite of George Washington and detested by Thomas Jefferson. He was a proponent of a strong central government, a sound fiscal policy, an author of *The Federalist Papers* which fought the battles of the Constitution in words, and the father of the Coast Guard. He was also a subject of scandal, and he died in a duel. Had he lived today, he would have been seen and heard on the Sunday morning news show circuit as well as in the tabloids. He might have appreciated the fact that for a long time, he has circulated in commerce as a form of currency. But if asked to name him or list his role in American history, many would be stumped. Hamilton did not shun the spotlight when he was alive and it's unfortunate that, in death, he is not more widely known.

In the Beginning

Born in the British West Indies to a married woman and the Scottish trader who was not her husband, Alexander Hamilton was probably born in 1755, but 1757 has also been suggested. Rachel Faucette (or Fawcett) Levine left her husband and moved with her lover, James Hamilton, to her birthplace of Nevis, where she gave birth to two sons, James, Jr., and Alexander. When James Hamilton abandoned her, Rachel became the support of her children by managing a store in St. Croix. When she died, the husband that she had left entered the picture and took her belongings, but a family friend bought back the books for Hamilton, whose reading was part of his education. Being born out of wedlock would have been an impediment for most youths at the time. Hamilton's illegitimate birth meant that he was not entitled to take part in the local school which was operated by the Church of England. But the intelligent boy's abilities did not go unnoticed.

Hamilton's love of reading refined his writing talents,

which in turn provided him with employable skills. He was working as a clerk at the age of 11 or 13, depending on which year of birth is considered. Fortunately, it was a time when talent could showcase itself and alter a young boy's destiny. An article that Hamilton wrote about a devastating hurricane that struck the town of Christiansted in 1772 attracted the attention of his employer and another local leader; together they raised the money to send Hamilton to the colony of New Jersey so that he could receive an education. He followed his time in grammar school with King's College, now Columbia University, but, as the fever of political thought inflamed the colonies, Hamilton caught the contagion. He wrote articles in support of independence and in 1775, joined a New York militia company. The students drilled before classes, but, on his own, Hamilton pursued a martial education as well, studying tactics and military history. In 1776, he raised a unit of soldiers and was elected captain of the New York Provincial Company of Artillery.

Hamilton Gets Noticed

Hamilton had a way of getting attention and his early success in his military efforts, which included action in the Battle of White Plains and the Battle of Trenton, made him a likely candidate to join the staffs of

American generals Nathaniel Greene or Henry Knox. He declined both officers but accepted General George Washington's offer to become his aide de camp. For four years, Hamilton oversaw Washington's correspondence, handling letters to Congress, governors, and generals; he negotiated with senior officers, dealt in diplomacy, and had his hand in intelligence.

Hamilton the Husband

Hamilton was well placed to meet people of influence. Philip Schuyler was influential in politics and military matters, as well as being socially well connected. By trade he was, like his friend George Washington, a surveyor by training. His second-eldest daughter Elizabeth was described as quietly intellectual. Called Betsey by Hamilton, she married the rising young New Yorker in 1780; together they would have eight children. Marriage to a Schuyler promoted Hamilton into the hierarchy of New York society. His choice of wife served Hamilton well; she copied the drafts of his writings so that they would be more legible. His wife would prove to be one of his most steadfast supporters, even during later years, when political turmoil and his sexual infidelities would have strained most marriages.

But Hamilton's innate abilities made him a person of note. Although he was illegitimate with the humblest of origins, he managed to build a friendship with the titled Marquis de Lafayette, who was also part of Washington's inner circle. But Hamilton also sought fame and saw no opportunity for it as long as he was merely the General's clerk. When Washington gave him command of an infantry battalion, Hamilton's military actions, combined with French fighting, played a part in the events which ultimately led to the surrender of the British at Yorktown.

Having earned military prestige, Hamilton was ready to return to civilian life and in 1782 was appointed as a representative from New York to the Congress of the Confederation, the precursor to what would eventually evolve into the legislative body of government. Like Washington, Hamilton had witnessed the impotence of a weak central government, which had no power to raise funds and was dependent upon the states, meaning that the Continental Army had not always been able to pay its soldiers or provide their needed supplies. The states wanted their independence, but they didn't want to be taxed by the government to pay for it.

Two incidents involving soldiers who had not received

their pay demonstrated the vulnerability of the government and could have created an insurrection which would have threatened the nation's future stability. Hamilton called for a revision to the weak Articles of Confederation which served as the country's form of government. Hamilton had given the subject a great deal of thought and his ideas would resurface at a later time; the resolution supported a powerful federal government, divided into three branches that would be able to raise taxes and an army.

Resigning from the Congress, Hamilton taught himself law and had a practice in New York City. His practice, which provided legal defense for former Loyalists and British subjects who were presenting claims for damages to the court, was thriving. Hamilton's defense of the Loyalists is regarded as a key factor in legal due process and the *Rutgers v. Waddington* case was a landmark in the creation of the judicial review system. He had not forgotten his passion for finance, however, and before the age of 30, he founded the Bank of New York, which is still in operation as the oldest bank in the United States.

Hamilton Takes the Stage

Forged in the fires of the American quest for independence, Hamilton's political instincts resurfaced. Many people recognized that the Articles of Confederation lacked the ability to give the government the power it needed to fuse 13 squabbling states into one cohesive nation. Hamilton could have told them exactly what the problem was: the government needed to be able to draw on a reliable and sustainable source of revenue. He had seen what this inability had done to the army led by Washington, where states unwilling to supply financial resources meant that soldiers went without pay and provisions.

As a delegate to the convention which met in Philadelphia in 1787 to solve this dilemma, Hamilton, along with James Madison and John Jay, was the author of the essays now known as *The Federalist Papers*, which were, in effect, a media lobbying effort to promote the ratification of the Constitution. Upon ratification, the document emerged as the law of the land in the United States.

The nation now had a government, and in 1789, it had a president. George Washington, mindful of Hamilton's fiscal acumen, named him to the post of first secretary of the treasury. Hamilton's task was to tackle the monumental debt that had arisen during the recent Revolutionary War. Hamilton was a proponent of a powerful central government, but not all Cabinet members shared this stance, fearing that a federal government could overreach its boundaries and encroach on the individual sovereignty of the states. Hampton proved his ability to negotiate when he promoted his intended policies to help the country establish credit with other countries, institute federal tax collection, have the federal government assume the states' debts, and initiate payment of federal war bonds. However, these proposals alarmed the states' rights contingent. At the same time, jockeying was in place to select a location for the country's national capital. Hamilton, bargaining with James Madison over dinner, reached a deal: Madison would refrain from presenting obstacles to a powerful central government that could proceed with the proposed fiscal policies. In exchange, Hamilton surrendered New York's interest in becoming the nation's capital.

If Hamilton had presidential aspirations, they did not come to fruition but he had only himself to blame. In 1797, Hamilton's dalliance with a married woman became public knowledge, creating a scandal that tainted his reputation beyond repair. The scandal was first publicized when a pamphlet was published that named Hamilton's mistress, Maria Reynolds, and connected him to a plot by her husband to illegally manipulate federal securities. Hamilton's method for demonstrating that he was innocent of financial misconduct, although not of marital infidelity, was to publish the letters he'd written to his married paramour.

Hamilton's relationship with Reynolds had begun with Hamilton in a beneficial role. A New Yorker herself, the 23-year old Reynolds had approached him when he was in Philadelphia for help because her husband had abandoned her. She wanted to return to New York so that she could be with her family and friends. When Hamilton returned to where she was staying with the money she needed, they ended up in her bedroom. The affair continued through the summer and fall of 1791. When James Reynolds came back into the picture, he wrote to Hamilton, accusing him of ruining a happy marriage. In exchange for $1,000, Reynolds said he would leave. But he remained in the city, the affair continued, and he continued to receive money from Hamilton. When Reynolds ended up in prison for committing forgery, he asked Hamilton for help. Hamilton refused, and Reynolds turned to Hamilton's enemies to let them know that he possessed information that could ruin the adulterous political leader.

Republican James Monroe learned the sordid tale

when he visited Reynolds in jail. The version that Monroe received labelled Hamilton as a scoundrel and a seducer. He didn't inform Monroe that he had requested money from Hamilton; instead, he said that his forgery and speculation plot involved Hamilton. Hamilton admitted to the affair, and Monroe agreed not to disclose what he knew. But Monroe made a copy of the letters the couple had exchanged and sent them to Thomas Jefferson. Hamilton and Jefferson were bitter enemies. Hamilton had made reference to Jefferson's own less-than-pristine private life; the rumors of Jefferson's sexual liaison with his slave, Sally Heming, were rife in political circles, but unproven. The letters were seen by others who opposed Hamilton's political stance. In 1797, the scandal was exposed. Hamilton's reputation was soiled, but more importantly, the accusation of financial misconduct that Reynolds had levied against him could imperil the Federalist Party which supported the fiscal policies Hamilton had promoted. He published *Observations on Certain Documents* with the intention of demonstrating his guilt as an adulterer but his innocence in any financial malfeasance, and his victimization at the hands of James Reynolds' extortion. Hamilton sacrificed his marital honor for the sake of his fiscal reputation. His wife not only forgave him, but she attempted to reverse the effects of the publication. She did not, however, forgive James Monroe for his role in the episode.

Hamilton was committed to the establishment of the United States as a nation founded upon the principles of liberty and financial stability. His role in establishing financial credibility for the new nation built a great foundation for its ongoing security. Hamilton had left the Treasury position in 1795, but remained deeply involved in politics. His involvement would kill him. The 1800 election for president had Thomas Jefferson and John Adams vying for the position. Aaron Burr, running for the office of vice president (the elections for the two offices were held separately at this time), tied Jefferson for the number of presidential votes. Hamilton chose to throw his considerable influence behind Jefferson, although the two were hardly in accord. The House of Representatives chose Jefferson as President and Burr as Vice President. But when Burr read that Hamilton had described him as "the most unfit and dangerous man of the community," Burr challenged Hamilton to a duel. There was already bad blood between the two. When Maria Reynolds sued her husband for divorced, her attorney was Aaron Burr.

It was not the first duel by a Hamilton. In 1801, in an attempt to defend his father's honor, Philip Hamilton was killed in a duel. That memory may have affected Alexander Hamilton's conduct when he and Burr met at dawn on July 11, 1804, in New Jersey. Whether or not he was reluctant to fire directly at his opponent, Hamilton's shot missed Burr, but Burr's aim was fatal; Hamilton died the following day from the wound.

Why was Hamilton Important?

It's interesting that, in the year when talk of adding a famous American woman to the ten-dollar bill has brought Alexander Hamilton back into the public conversation, the musical version of the Founding Father has found success on Broadway. Los Angeles Times reporter Charles McNulty asked the following question in his review of the musical: "How does (the composer) connect audiences to characters separated by more than 200 years, funny costumes and vastly different imperatives? By relating the hopes and setbacks, squabbles and seductions, triumphs and tragedies, of these 18th century American rebels in a score that allows the past to speak in the musical language of the rebellious present—rap." The musical demonstrates the essence of Hamilton, the immigrant who overcame poverty and hardship to become one of the foundational beams of the nation. The essence of

Hamilton is, of course, the essence of America. Hamilton had a keen intuition about the country he cherished, and he understood what it needed in a way that perhaps none of the other Founding Fathers could. His poverty and illegitimacy could have made him an outsider; in the other, established countries of power, it probably would have. But in a new nation, Hamilton could climb to the heights of power, and by doing so, he left his mark on his adoptive country.

With European influences still so prevalent in the Americas, the United States was not yet strong enough to challenge other governments. Hamilton's intention was to make the nation internally strong by developing a solid financial infrastructure. Hamilton's morality in terms of marital fidelity was flawed, but in his view, the nation's moral character depended upon being able to honor the debts it had contracted in its fight for independence. He also wanted Americans to become accustomed to handling money, and his ideas for the establishment of the U.S. Mint were adopted by Congress in 1792. His perception that the nation needed a system of defense for the protection of the Eastern coast to protect against piracy and control smuggling led to the establishment of what would eventually become the United States Coast Guard. He was a man of varied interests, but his practical approach to nation building constructed a sustainable root system which has reaped a harvest of prosperity.

Perhaps the lyrics of the musical are the best way to understand Alexander Hamilton:

"The 10-dollar Founding Father without a father
Got a lot farther by working a lot harder,
By being a lot smarter . . .
By being a self-starter."

Chapter 3 - Benjamin Franklin: The First American

Who was Benjamin Franklin?

Benjamin Franklin lived in a time of limited communication, but none of the Founding Fathers was better able to serve as his own press agent than the multitasking Philadelphian whose talents are so enormous that he must be regarded as America's original Renaissance Man. He was a tradesman who made his living as a printer, but he was also a politician who helped to negotiate the treaty that ended the war with Great Britain. He left school at the age of ten but received honorary degrees from Harvard, Yale, Oxford, and the University of St. Andrews. He was a printer by trade but an inventor by inclination; the Franklin stove, bifocals, and the lightning rod are his. As an amateur scientist, his experiments with electricity received attention in England with the publication of articles on his work. He was a dedicated civic citizen and philanthropist, creating Philadelphia's first lending

44

library and the city's volunteer fire department. He supported the independence of the 13 colonies and worked with his Southern counterparts, but freed his own two slaves when he committed himself to the abolitionist movement in opposition of slavery.

He was a man of morals who had a common-law marriage and had fathered an illegitimate son. He's as famous for the moral guidance in *Poor Richard's Almanack* as he is for the bon mots and flirtatious comments he exchanged with the ladies in France. Contradictions? Perhaps, but Benjamin Franklin lived to be 84, and into those years he crammed the events and accomplishments of a dozen men. Not all his personalities played by conventional rules. It was the ability to adroitly know when to be shrewd, and when to be honorable, that made him such a remarkable human being who recalibrated the definition of what it meant to be an American at a time when colonials were often regarded as bumpkins and buffoons. No one could relegate Benjamin Franklin to inferior status and his stature gave luster to his country.

In the Beginning

Born in 1706, the 15th of 17 children of a soap and candle maker, Benjamin Franklin did not attract Boston's attention as the man who would one day be famous in the most sophisticated world capitals. His father originally intended his young son to be a member of the clergy, so at the age of eight, young Benjamin was sent to the South Grammar School. In his autobiography, Franklin referred to this humorously when he wrote that he was his father's tithe to the church. The Franklins were a religious family with Puritan beliefs, but their young son, although he endorsed the traits of hard work and helping others which the Puritans preached, did not display a particularly religious personality. The ambition to be a minister belonged to Josiah Franklin, not to his son.

But with so many children to provide for, funding for education was not available and he was taken out of school after a few months. He went to another school for a year, but that was the end of his formal schooling. At the age of ten, he was taken out of school and put to work with his father. When candle making failed to command the boy's attention, his father let him explore his career options by watching other Boston tradesmen, but nothing appealed to him. He thought he wanted to go to sea. That wasn't to Josiah Franklin's liking; his older son, also named Josiah, had followed that ambition and had never returned home to Boston, so he apprenticed Benjamin to his brother James, a printer.

This was more to the boy's liking. Franklin was a voracious reader and a print shop offered a world of opportunities for a 12-year old who was intelligent, eager to learn and willing to work. Benjamin was signed up for a nine-year indenture. His brother's *The New England Courant*, which had been started in 1721, was innovative; although Boston had two other newspapers, they reprinted news from abroad. But James Franklin's newspapers included shipping schedules, opinion pieces, articles, and advertisements with original content rather than a repeat of what was going on across the Atlantic. In some ways, perhaps James Franklin's publication was in the forefront of a new brand of American journalism that may have influenced his younger brother.

However, James Franklin was not eager to embrace an apprentice who had a talent with words. Franklin was determined to improve his writing and he bought a copy of the popular London magazine, the *Spectator*, and studied the magazine as if it were his textbook, rewriting the essays in his own words so that he would learn to write well. His passion for reading was undiminished, and at the age of 16, he decided to become a vegetarian because simple meals—boiled potatoes, rice, hasty pudding, bread, raisins, and water to drink—took less time, leaving more time for books. Franklin tried his hand at writing but his brother hadn't taken on a writer for an apprentice and he refused to publish Franklin's work. But Franklin found a way to get his work into print. Readers were soon entertained to read letters submitted by Mrs. Silence Dogood in *The New England Courant*, but James was furious when he discovered, some 16 letters later, that Mrs. Dogood was in reality his younger brother. Mrs. Silence Dogood was indeed silenced after James discovered her identity.

The brothers ran afoul of the Mathers, the influential Puritan clergymen, when they opposed inoculation against smallpox, which was a deadly and disfiguring disease. James Franklin mocked the clergymen for their stance, and his irreverence offended Bostonians. It would be one of the few times when Benjamin Franklin adopted an incorrect scientific viewpoint; inoculation was an effective means of prevention against getting the disease, one that George Washington would advocate for his soldiers when the war began. When the elder Franklin was jailed for his views, Benjamin managed the printing of the newspaper. Unfortunately, sibling rivalry trumped gratitude. Tired of his mistreatment, Benjamin Franklin ran away from Boston.

He boarded a ship that took him to New York, but he couldn't find work as a printer. Having run out on his apprenticeship, which was a legal contract, Franklin was in an ambiguous situation with no master printer to vouch for him. He traveled across New Jersey, eventually arriving in Philadelphia. He was travel-worn, unkempt, and carrying rolls that he'd bought with his remaining funds. His failure to create a good impression didn't stand in the way of his future, however, although a young woman named Deborah Read did see him and thought that he was a very odd-looking young man, carrying his belongings and his roles and showing the evidence of his rustic travel. He took lodgings at the Read home in 1723, and he and Deborah began courting. But even Philadelphia was too confining for the curious Franklin and the following year he went to London to work again as a printer.

When he returned to Philadelphia in 1726, Deborah had married. Franklin was not celibate, nor was he married; he sired a son named William, born outside of wedlock in 1727. Several years later Franklin was elected as Pennsylvania's official printer, and purchased *The Pennsylvania Gazette* from a previous employer. Deborah Read became Deborah Franklin in

1730, although theirs was a common-law marriage; her first husband had disappeared, his whereabouts was unknown. If she was a widow, she didn't know it and the couple opted for marriage that might possibly have been bigamy. Publishing *Poor Richard's Almanack*, inventing the Franklin stove (for which he refused to take out a patent because his invention was designed to help others by providing a more heat-efficient means of keeping people warm in cold weather), and joining the Pennsylvania militia all kept the husband and father busy and made him a wealthy man.

Franklin Gets Noticed

In the beginning, he entered politics to represent the colony of Pennsylvania, traveling to England as a representative of the state in a dispute with the Penn family, the original founders of the colony. He went to England as an Englishman, but in his homeland, thoughts of independence were stirring. The colonists were infuriated by the Stamp Act which Parliament passed to recoup some of the money spent on the French and Indian War. Franklin appeared before Parliament to speak against the law, which was eventually repealed. But the thoughts of independence, incited even more by his growing sense of distance from what Great Britain had become, with its entrenched political leadership and rigid social structure, made him begin to ponder independence.

When he returned home, his allegiances belonged to the Patriots who supported separation from the mother country. The issue of independence became a family source of conflict; his son William was loyal to Britain and served as the royal governor of the colony of New Jersey. The breach between father and son would never be mended. But Franklin's ties to his daughter Sarah, who was called Sally, the product of his marriage to Deborah, were strong and affectionate. And humorously candid. In one letter, he admitted to her that, in his opinion, the eagle had not been chosen as the symbol of the United States. Franklin was of the view that the eagle was a bird of bad moral character that was lazy and instead of finding his own food, was all too fond of stealing the prey caught by other birds. Franklin felt this to be an unsuitable representative of an industrious country.

Franklin the Ladies' Man

Firmly ensconced in the separation movement, Franklin went to Paris as the colonies' ambassador and spent almost ten years there. His time in France built his reputation as a man of letters and intellect, and Franklin played his part well. He dressed the part of a backwoods American, but conducted himself with the sophistication of a cosmopolitan. Franklin found the amorous atmosphere of the French amendable. Now a widower since the death of his wife in 1774, Franklin enjoyed the attention of the ladies and they were quite willing to flirt in response. He sent love letters to a married woman and proposed marriage to a widow, Madame Helvetius. He enjoyed the intellectual gifts of the French ladies as well, discussing politics with the Duchess de La Rochefoucauld while capitalizing on the influence of the Countess d'Houdetot, a supporter of the American quest for independence.

His friendship with the married Madame Brillon gave him the opportunity to employ his writing skills with his political deftness. His "Treaty of Peace" was written in a political tone and mixed flirtation and companionship. In Article 4 of the Treaty, Franklin wrote that when he was with Madame Brillion, he would drink tea, play chess, hear music, or do anything she required of him. Later, in Article 8, he wrote that he would do what he pleases when he was with her, but later in the conclusion of the treaty, he admitted that he had little hope that she would consent to it.

Not all of his social engagements were romantic in nature. He met with many in France who were opposed to slavery and formed a lifelong friendship with the Marquis de Condorcet, who is regarded as a pioneer of modern social science. Cordorcet had bold ideas about equality and formed an abolitionist society. Franklin's opposition to slavery was shared by Dr. Benjamin Rush, a Patriot and the two would join forces to form an abolitionist society in 1787.

Franklin Takes the Stage

He was part of the committee that worked on the Declaration of Independence. Although the writing was done by Thomas Jefferson, Franklin did help to edit the early versions of the document. At the signing of the Declaration, a treasonous act in the eyes of the British, Franklin famously said, "Yes, we must indeed all hang together, or most assuredly, we shall all hang separately."

It was not for Franklin to lead troops; he was already an old man by this time. But his country benefitted by his civilian experience. Franklin had previously served as the postmaster of Philadelphia and had implemented innovations which improved the speed of mail service. In 1775, when the United States Post Office was established by the Second Continental Congress, Benjamin Franklin was named the country's first Postmaster General.

Franklin's warm ties with the French, combined with the American military victory at the Battle of Saratoga, helped to convince the French to ally themselves with the rebellious colonials. They provided loans to help finance the war, funds which were desperately needed because the American government had no sustained means of raising revenue from the individual states, which tended to be stingy with their funds.

French support, combined with Washington's leadership and American determination, finally defeated the British. Franklin signed the Treaty of Paris ending the war in 1783, and returned home. But his work wasn't finished, although he was well into his 70s. The business of writing a Constitution summoned him to the Constitutional Convention in his home city of Philadelphia in 1787. His contributions were minimal as the debate was carried on by the younger delegates, but his presence solidified his stature as a human cornerstone to American independence. Franklin is the sole Founding Father who signed the four major documents that created the United States: the Declaration of Independence, the Treaty of Alliance with the French; the Treaty of Paris which ended the American Revolution; and the United States Constitution.

Franklin's contributions to his country are indisputably of note; in every endeavor, he seemed to be intent on making life better for others. He invented bifocal glasses to help people with vision problems. He invented the lightning rod, swim fins, the glass harmonica and even the urinary catheter. His creation of the catheter was inspired by the suffering his brother John endured from kidney stones. Catheters existed but they were bulky. Franklin's version was a thin, silver tube that was inserted into the urethra so that urine could drain from the bladder. As with the Franklin stove, he made no effort to obtain patents for his invention. They were his gift to the public. He explained his reasoning in his autobiography, writing "As we enjoy great advantages from the inventions of others, we should be glad of an opportunity to serve others by any invention of ours, and this we should do freely and generously." Although Franklin may not have followed the traditional religious themes of the era, he nonetheless believed in taking care of others, and making his community a better place to live.

But he was no less vital to the annals of the state in which he lived. According to a Harper poll, 67% of Pennsylvanians named Benjamin Franklin as the state's greatest citizen. As a Philadelphian, he founded the first lending library in the country. An avid reader himself, he wanted books, which were scarce in the colonies as well as costly, to be available to others. Members of his Library Company, founded in 1731, could afford to buy books from England to share with others. The Library Company of Philadelphia has a collection of half a million books and personal items that belonged to Franklin, as well as first editions of American classics Moby Dick and *Leaves of Grass*.

He formed a group of people who created the Pennsylvania Hospital in 1751 so that Philadelphia could take better care of its sick. Thanks to him, the first learned society in the country, the American Philosophical Society, was created. What's even more amazing about these developments is that they're still in existence now, centuries later.

In 1736, Franklin organized the Philadelphia Union Fire Company, the first in the city, because fire was such a prevalent threat. Going further, he helped to found the Philadelphia Contribution for Insurance Against Loss by Fire, so that people who took out insurance policies would not be financially ruined if their property was damaged by fire. Franklin's contributions to Philadelphia society have a long shelf life: the insurance company is still operating today.

Franklin's reformer instincts were aroused by slavery, the prevailing controversy of the developing country. At one time, he had owned two slaves; in early colonial America, slavery existed in the North and South and was largely accepted as part of the colonies' economic structure. Originally, Franklin shared the views of his fellow countrymen in believing that African slaves were intellectually inferior to the European settlers. But when he visited a school that taught young African children in 1763, he noted that they were inferior to no one. The abolition movement was just getting started, but when Franklin returned home from France in 1785, he became president of an abolitionist group that had been founded by Quakers. He freed his slaves, and proposed the idea that in order to contribute to a free society, slaves needed to be educated. He perceived that traits which slaves were criticized for were actually the result of their enslaved environment rather than any lack of ability. But when the issue of slavery was undergoing debate in the Constitutional Convention, Franklin did not speak up on behalf of slaves. No one is sure why, but many wonder if, when Franklin revealed in a speech that he didn't entirely approve of the Constitution, it was because of the document's tolerance of enslavement.

Franklin died at the age of 84 in 1790; Philadelphia

mourned the passing of its celebrated citizen, and 20,000 people attended his funeral. The self-educated son of a Boston candle maker had used his talents to help invent a new country, one which was as unique and practical as any of his own inventions.

Why was Franklin Important?

When author Stephen Covey was planning his book, *The 7 Habits of Highly Effective People*, he studied Franklin's habits for the example the Founding Father provided. Franklin was an early success story for a country that had been settled by what the Old World regarded as its discards. In an era when the American colonies seemed to be teeming with talented leaders who could take their young, raw country to a new level of political opportunity, Benjamin Franklin was the first among equals. He had old-fashioned virtues and a contemporary brilliance that made him at home whether he was promoting one of his plans for the betterment of Philadelphia or speaking as a statesman in front of the French court. His experiments in science, his dedication to education with the establishment of the University of Pennsylvania, his inventions, his commitment to philanthropy, and his opposition to slavery, all marked him as a man of conscience. Politically, he stamped his mark on the nation that would grow from a wild frontier to a preeminent player on the world stage.

But he also contributed to society in a way that had nothing to do with his work as an American or a Pennsylvanian. His biographer, Walter Isaacson, himself a journalist, proposed the idea that Franklin's success as the publisher of the *Pennsylvania Gazette* proved his intention to broaden the partisan journalism of his era by considering multiple sides of an issue. In that respect, Franklin's style served as a forerunner of modern news coverage. Franklin followed up on his support of the First Amendment. "Franklin is one of the first American publishers," Isaacson explained, "to understand that freedom of the press and tolerance are part of what it is to be a newspaper editor, and what it is to be a printer. And part of the genius of America is that we're open in our discourse." Franklin espoused the cause of truth, even when it was unpopular and opposed the prevailing viewpoint of society. That foundational bedrock of truth as the ultimate arbiter of a newspaper's content has defended journalists centuries after Franklin's days as a publisher.

Isaacson goes on to say that "Franklin was the best diplomat of his age, the best scientist, the best writer, the best inventor, the most practical politician and the great civic leader. Nobody today can come close to doing all of that."

Chapter 4 - Abraham Lincoln: The Savior of the Union

Who was Abraham Lincoln?

Conventional wisdom holds that if gangly, homely, rough-edged Abraham Lincoln were running for national office in today's cosmetic political environment, he'd never get elected. The truth is that the Kentucky-born Westerner wasn't reckoned to have much of a chance of getting elected anyway, and had the country not been so splintered by North-South factionalism, it's unlikely that he'd have won the White House. Nonetheless, his presidential victory was perceived as the ultimate insult to the Southern states, who interpreted his election as their clarion call to secession. What they didn't know was that while Abraham Lincoln wasn't prepared to go to war over slavery, he was not prepared to allow the country to be sliced in half. This enigmatic man who steered the country through its bloodiest war has become an American icon. The truth is that he was entirely flesh and blood, prone to depression and doubt, enduring family tragedies that were almost beyond endurance.

Being president ultimately did end his life at the hands of an assassin, but Lincoln is regarded as the man who saved the Union.

In the Beginning

One of America's most eloquent presidents probably received less than a total of 18 months of formal education. He was born in 1809 on the Kentucky frontier, where back-breaking work was plentiful, and books scarce. His mother, Nancy Hanks Lincoln, died when he was young; Lincoln was devoted to his mother, but also developed a strong tie to his stepmother, Sarah Bush Lincoln, after his father Thomas married her. Although Lincoln and his father were not close, the youth was fortunate that his stepmother supported his love of books. But books were for leisure; it was with an ax that Lincoln made his living after he went on his own.

Lincoln was not particularly fond of hard physical labor, and when he moved to Illinois, he switched to less strenuous work as a postmaster and store owner. He had a commanding presence, standing a towering 6'4", and demonstrated a genial, winning way with people. He was elected the leader of a group of volunteers when war broke out with the Black Hawk tribe in 1832. While many politicians are guilty of enhancing their military experience, Lincoln's customary sense of humor did the opposite. As the captain of the Illinois volunteers, he conceded that the troops did not engage in combat, except for "a good many bloody struggles with the mosquitoes."

In 1834, he was elected to the Illinois State Legislature. He also taught himself the law and was admitted to the bar in 1836. When he moved to Springfield, Illinois, he and William Herndon became law partners. His practice prospered but his political career seemed to be running out of steam and after one term in the House of Representatives, he decided not to run for a second term. His romantic interests traveled a somewhat rocky road: there was the reported romance with Ann Rutledge in New Salem, who died of typhoid of fever, leaving Lincoln devastated, or perhaps not; historians are dubious that this was the love of his life.

Lincoln the Husband

Mary Todd was from Lexington, and her wealthy, slave-owning family neighbored Henry Clay, the American political titan. When she was ten years old, she rode to the Clay estate to show him her new pony. Years later when she went to Springfield, Illinois, where her sister, who had married the son of the former governor of Illinois, lived, she probably met Lincoln, a rising political star on the scene. Senator Stephen Douglas, who would later figure in Lincoln's future, was a suitor of the Kentucky belle. Mary Todd was not like most women of the era; she had a superior education, having spent 10 years at the Shelby Female Academy. As an adult, she was well informed on the political events of that tumultuous time. She saw something in the lanky frontier lawyer, and the two became engaged.

His engagement ended a year after it was announced, and then turned into marriage a year after that. Lincoln was 33 years old, Mary Todd a decade younger. The couple may have realized early on that their natures were not designed for tranquil matrimony, but the union produced four sons. While Lincoln was away from home as an Illinois circuit lawyer, his wife was along for long stretches of time and the responsibility of managing the household and raising their sons fell upon her. For eldest son Robert, his father was remembered as someone who was always getting ready to go somewhere.

The Lincolns were indulgent parents but their family was destined for tragedy. Only eldest son Robert lived into adulthood; Willie died in 1862 while his father was president. Eddie died in 1850 and Tad in 1871. Any mother would be emotionally affected by the deaths of her children, and for Mary Todd Lincoln, the loss of her sons played its part in her volatile mental health. The couple's happiest days were when they lived in Springfield, Illinois

Lincoln Gets Noticed

Since its founding, the nation had tried to deal with the issue of slavery by effecting legislative compromises that simply avoided the problem instead of confronting it. The South was politically very powerful with representatives in Congress who were adept at maintaining the institution of slavery. Americans knew that one day, the question would have to be resolved. By the 1850s, the delicate balancing act between slave and free states was challenging even the nation's most talented politicians. A new political party, the Republican Party, arose when Congress passed the Kansas-Nebraska Act which allowed individual states and new territories to decide on their own whether they would permit slavery. The Republican Party was opposed to slavery and in its rise to national prominence, Abraham Lincoln found his appetite for politics whetted. When he challenged Senator Stephen Douglas for his Senate seat in 1858, the debates between the candidates drew crowds and extensive media coverage. When he was nominated as the Republican candidate, Lincoln delivered his historic "House Divided" speech which, to many, predicted the split which was doomed to happen: "A house divided against itself cannot stand. I believe this government cannot endure permanently half slave and half free. I do not expect the Union to be dissolved—I do not expect the house to fall—but I do expect it will cease to be divided. It will become all one thing, or all the other."

Lincoln lost that election, but he'd made a name for himself on the national stage. The issue of slavery was 19th century America's equivalent of a reality show, and citizens watched in riveting suspense as North and South battled for legislative supremacy. The South believed that secession was an inherent right of the states because the federal government did not have the right to coerce any state into remaining in the union if it chose to leave. In his memoirs of the Civil War, Jefferson Davis, who would serve as the first and only president of the Confederacy, cited numerous examples earlier in the country's history when Northern states threatened to secede because of displeasure with legislative rulings. President Buchanan, Lincoln's predecessor, did not believe that the president could prevent a state from seceding;

some of his inertia in the weeks before he left office stemmed from this conviction.

The presidential campaign of 1860 was a circus, as the North and South each elected their own candidates. Lincoln was the Republican candidate, besting William Seward and Salmon Chase for the nomination. He would later name both men to his Cabinet.

Serious as the circumstances were, Lincoln's rise to presidential status owed something to an 11-year old girl named Grace Bedell. Grace, a New Yorker, wrote the president to say that she thought the clean-shaven Lincoln would have a better chance of winning the election if he grew a beard. Lincoln responded to her letter, but didn't promise that he would do as she suggested. However, by the time he began the journey from Illinois to Washington D.C., he had a beard. When he stopped in New York, he met the girl who had inspired his changed look. Lincoln left the train car and moved through the crowd to greet her and give her a kiss before saying good-bye. The crowd was delighted by this informal meeting between a president and one of their own.

Lincoln Takes the Stage

There were rumors that conspirators had plans to

assassinate the newly elected president before he was inaugurated. Allan Pinkerton of the famed Pinkerton National Detective Agency was in charge of Lincoln's security during the journey to the capital, and he believed that Lincoln was in danger. Pinkerton had the telegraph lines to Baltimore cut so that potential conspirators between Pennsylvania and Maryland would not be able to communication. When he arrived in Harrisburg, Lincoln left the city on a special train that took him to Baltimore very late at night. Baltimore did not permit nighttime railroad traffic in the downtown area, meaning that the rail cars would need to be drawn by horses for that segment of the journey.

The decision made Lincoln look like a coward in the eyes of the nation, especially since there was no conclusive proof that the conspiracy had really existed. Lincoln's many enemies reveled in the tale and it was certainly a humiliating way for a presidency to begin, especially at a time when so many people all over the world were closely watching how the unknown Lincoln would perform in the office.

He received 40 percent of the popular vote, but it was enough. The Republicans won the White House. The die was cast. The news that an anti-slavery candidate had won the White House spurred the Southern states into secession; by the time Lincoln was inaugurated in March, 1861, the Union had seven fewer states. Lincoln had made no declarations that he would do anything about slavery and he didn't want the states to secede. Perhaps no president has ever faced a more conflicted start to his first term in office. Southern hostility turned to gunfire when the Confederate troops fired on Fort Sumter in South Carolina. Whether Lincoln wanted war or not was no longer an issue; the North was at war with the South, and the South had fired the first shots.

As a Kentuckian, Mary Todd Lincoln was regarded with suspicion by many in Washington, although she was committed to Lincoln's political policies. She had family members who served in the Confederate Army; several were killed in battle. But the country at war did not see her as one of them; she was a Westerner, and they regarded her as backward and coarse, despite her education. She suffered from migraines and depression, leading modern historians to believe that she may have been a victim of bipolar disorder. A head injury that she suffered in a carriage accident made the symptoms worse. Another trait which angered her husband was her spending sprees. The country which was enduring privation because of the war was not tolerant of a president's wife who refurbished the

White House and purchased new china. Congress appropriated funds to pay the expenses, but Mary Todd Lincoln's spending also extended to her personal wardrobe, and her husband was not always aware of the expenses she incurred. In a time of national tensions, the Lincoln White House endured domestic friction as well, compounded by tragedy when their son Willie died of typhoid fever in 1862.

Robert Todd Lincoln, the eldest son, was the only one of their offspring to survive into the 20th century. He had an often troubled relationship with his parents. His mother refused to allow him to enlist in the Union Army despite the president's understanding that other families were just as fearful that their sons would be killed as Mary Todd Lincoln was for their son. Finally, as the war was ending, she surrendered her objections and Robert Lincoln left Harvard Law School to serve on General Grant's staff.

Between family tensions and political strife, Lincoln faced tremendous opposition during the early years of the war. His cabinet was comprised of, as historian Doris Kearns Goodwin's book terms it, a *Team of Rivals*; several of his Cabinet members had sought his job, and were often disparaging of the president's ability to govern. Had the Union army been able to notch victories, his political path might have been smoother, but Lincoln struggled to find a general who would commit the troops to battle and to win. General George McClellan was popular with his troops, but contemptuous of the Commander-in-Chief. He drilled the army well and often, but was convinced that he always faced superior numbers and was reluctant to engage. At one point, Lincoln said, "If General McClellan does not want to use the army, I would like to borrow it for a time." McClellan's disdain for the president was well known; his references to Lincoln as a gorilla and baboon (insults which were often used against the president) were indicative of his views that he was serving an incompetent president who was his intellectual inferior.

Lincoln needed military victories. The Confederate Army was lobbying for Great Britain to recognize them. The Battle of Antietam was fought on 1862, the bloodiest day in the history of America's wars. While it wasn't much of a victory, it gave Lincoln the credibility he needed to issue the Emancipation Proclamation five days after the battle. The Proclamation would go into effect on January 1, 1863 and would free the slaves located in the Southern states which were in rebellion against the Union. Bringing the issue of slavery to the forefront of the war was a strategic move that persuaded the European powers, notably Great Britain and France, not to recognize the Confederate States of America.

The year 1863 was a turning point in the war. On July 1, General Lee's Confederate Army crossed into Pennsylvania, the first time that the Southern forces had entered Northern territory. The Confederates were looking for shoes; what ensued was what many historians regard as the pivotal battle of the entire war. For three days, Union and Confederate forces battled at sites that have become memorable even to non-history buffs: Devil's Den; Little Round Top; Culp's Hill; Cemetery Hill; the Wheat Field; the Peach Orchard. During Pickett's Charge, 12,000 Virginians led a charge into Union fire; of those troops, 7500 were killed.

General Meade was credited with the victory, but he failed to pursue Lee's defeated troops, which headed back to Virginia. Meade was a cautious general and his troops were tired, but Lincoln was angry at Meade's failure to continue the battle. The war, he felt, could have ended in Gettysburg. But in November, when he dedicated the battlefield as a military cemetery, Lincoln's speech held no rancor. In a brief, two-minute delivery, he uttered phrases which have resonated through the years: "Fourscore and seven years ago, our fathers brought forth on this continent a new nation, conceived in liberty and dedicated to the proposition that all men are created equal"; "The world will little note, nor long remember, what we say here, but can never forget what they did here"; and "Government of the people, by the people, for the people." These phrases tell the story of the United States; its origins and its political foundation. Lincoln's two minutes of eloquence were much briefer than the two-hour oration offered by the celebrated Edward Everett, but Lincoln underestimated the endurance of the speech. The world long remembered what was said at the Gettysburg Cemetery.

McClellan was relieved of command, and promptly announced his candidacy for president in the 1864 election. He was popular, the war was not, and Lincoln was convinced that he would be defeated. But while military victories were slow in coming in the East, the West was a different matter. General Grant was winning battles; the cost in casualties was horrific, but with the tide turning, Lincoln felt that victory was possible. Lincoln was elected to a second term in the 1864 election. By the end of the year, General Sherman had captured Atlanta; by April of the following year, Richmond, the capital of the

Confederacy, had fallen. On April 9, 1865, Robert E. Lee surrendered his Confederate forces to General Grant.

Lincoln's determination to bring the South back into the Union with moderation rather than recrimination was opposed by the more radical members of his party, who believed that Reconstruction policies should punish the South for its transgressions. Much remained to be decided; winning the military battles was only a part of the solution to the country's post-Civil War issues. Lincoln had much on his mind. But he had been re-elected, the North had won the war, and the Union would be restored.

On April 14, Lincoln awakened in a cheerful mood, and why not? The war was over, Lincoln had been re-elected, and the future looked promising. That night, the Lincolns attended a play at Ford's Theatre; he and his wife held hands during the performance. The theatre was crowded as Washington's residents enjoy an evening without war anxiety hanging over them. Lincoln was a dedicated playgoer and with the war resolved, it must have seemed a good opportunity to relax. But John Wilkes Booth, a Southern sympathizer and an actor, knew of the Lincoln plans and was in the theatre. When Lincoln's bodyguard left the president's box during the intermission, Booth entered the box and shot the president. Booth then leaped from the president's box to the stage, ran across it, and escaped on a waiting horse. Some spectators heard him cry out "Sic semper tyrannis" as he left the box; others heard him cry out "The South shall be free! I have done it! Virginia is avenged" as he made his escape from the theatre.

Mayhem ensued. One of the actors described the scene in the theatre as "an inextricable chaos of mad humanity (swirling) hither and thither in historical aimlessness. . . no one seemed to have retained a scintilla of self-possession." Small wonder; the nation had just emerged victorious from the bloodiest war in America's history and through the duration of hostilities, they had feared the invasion of the Southern troops. With the war won, who in the audience would have expected to witness bloodshed on that night, or have expected the president to be the victim?

Lincoln died the following day. Son Robert stayed by his father's side as Lincoln's life ebbed, but Mary Todd Lincoln was ordered from the deathbed by Secretary of War Stanton because of her emotional expression of grief. The train bearing Lincoln's body traveled 1600 miles from Washington D.C. back home to Springfield, Illinois. During the 20-day journey, grieving citizens from cities along the route left their homes and businesses to pay their final respects to the fallen president Also in the car with Lincoln was the body of his son Willie, who had died in 1862. At each stop, an honor guard left the train to carry Lincoln's coffin to a designated viewing area. When the train journeyed at night, bonfires were lit so that the public could see despite the darkness.

The deaths of her sons and the assassination of her husband forever haunted Mary Todd Lincoln's remaining years. When Tad Lincoln died in 1871, Robert Lincoln felt that she was a danger to herself and had her committed to a psychiatric hospital in Illinois. But Mary had allies who supported her efforts to prove that she was sane. Mary escaped from the institution and her case attracted media attention. The resulting estrangement between mother and son was never healed.

Robert Lincoln had his own hauntings to deal with. He had been invited to attend the performance at Ford's Theatre on the night when his father was assassinated, but declined. He was an eyewitness to the assassination of President James Garfield, and was present at the Pan-American Exposition in 1901 when President McKinley was shot. Lincoln was aware of his morbid connection to history and at one point declined a presidential invitation because of what he described as a "certain fatality" when he was present during presidential events.

Why was Lincoln Important?

Much is made, and deservedly so, of Lincoln's commitment to the preservation of the Union. In order to do that, he had to transform the role of the president in a way that, to many people, violated the Constitution and exceeded the boundaries of his office. By combining his role as commander-in-chief during wartime with his role as the nation's chief executive, Lincoln's power surpassed that of the legislative and judicial branches. After Fort Sumter was fired upon and hostilities were launched, he entered the country into war without summoning Congress in advance. He called out the state militias, expanded the military, spent $2 million without Congressional appropriation, suspended habeas corpus, arrested suspected traitors whose dissent was regarded as treason, and in 1863, issued the Emancipation Proclamation. To Lincoln, he had been elected president to do what was required when a national emergency required swift action. He felt that the president's role superseded the authority of the other branches when the nation needed an executive in charge. Congress and the Supreme Court swear to support the Constitution; the president takes an oath to preserve, protect, and defend the Constitution. The power that Lincoln commanded would not be retained by subsequent presidents, but other presidents did not face the splitting of the nation.

For all the concrete instances of Lincoln's legacy, there is one that's more abstract. It's been noted that, prior to the Civil War, the United States was often referred to in the plural sense which reflected the nation's status as the combined total of individual states. After the war concluded, and the Union was restored, the plural reference ceased. The United States is, not are; the states which make up the country are part of a whole, and the whole is greater than the sum of its parts. That clarification is more than a matter of semantics. Throughout the war, Lincoln saw the country as one entity, and he was committed to fighting the battles because he could not sanction the separation of the states. He did not fight the war to free the slaves, but the Union victory accomplished their emancipation. His phenomenal vision held intact a belief in the United States as what he called "the last best hope of earth." It would be up to subsequent

78

generations of nations to fulfill that destiny. Lincoln, by holding fast to his vision of the United States as one country through travail and war, is responsible for its name holding true: the regions and states that make up the nation are truly the United States.

Chapter 5 - Theodore Roosevelt: The Bully Pulpit President

Who was Teddy Roosevelt?

Of all the American presidents, it's perhaps Theodore "Teddy" Roosevelt whose gusto for life transformed the presidency into his image, rather than the office altering him. He was a man for whom being president was merely one of the ways in which he made his mark upon his era. A reformer, a governor, a soldier, an environmentalist before the concept was mainstream, and a Nobel Peace Prize winner, TR's zest for living life to the fullest revealed the metamorphosis of a man who, as a child, was sickly and asthmatic. The future president handcrafted his destiny from an early age, adopting a physical fitness routine to force health to come to him and from that moment on, he believed that he could cure the ills of a country that simply needed to acknowledge its strengths rather than its weaknesses. He was vaulted into the White House because of the assassination in 1901 of President

William McKinley, making him the youngest man to assume the office of president. The power brokers did not expect the New York reformer to be anything more than the mostly invisible Vice President, but Theodore Roosevelt was not one to live his life unnoticed.

In the Beginning

Theodore Roosevelt, of the Oyster Bay Roosevelts, was born in 1858. His father was a successful businessman, his mother a Southern woman. Because his wife was distraught at the idea of her husband taking arms against her countrymen in the Civil War, Theodore Roosevelt, the father, paid a substitute to fight for him. It was a common and indeed a legal practice at the time, but when the son was older, he was bothered by his father's failure to serve, and his own military zeal was ignited by his father's choice to sit out the war. The robust, active president started out life as a sickly child who did not attend school because of his ailments. Although he was delicate, he was not a dull child; his early hobby of taxidermy meant that he and his cousins started their own museum with animals they had stuffed. Despite the limitations of his homeschooled education, he was a voracious reader and was inspired by biographies of those who had faced adversity and overcome it. Their heroic lives affected the psyche of the timid boy; when TR entered his teens, he began boxing and lifting weights to build up his physical stamina. Roosevelt was determined to overcome his physical weakness and his success at doing so made him a proponent of a vigorous and energetic life.

Theodore Roosevelt the Husband

While a student at Harvard, Roosevelt met Alice Hathaway Lee. The couple courted for 15 months. He graduated magna cum laude from Harvard, entered law school, and married her. Law school failed to hold his interest and he left, later becoming the youngest man to serve in the New York State Assembly, where he eventually became the minority leader.

Then tragedy struck on February 14, 1884; his wife died of kidney disease two days after giving birth; 11 hours before that, his mother had died of typhoid fever. Bereft, Roosevelt sought solace out West, living the life of a cattle rancher while his elder sister Bamie took care of his infant daughter Alice. TR never discussed the tragedies that had struck him; in his diary entry for that day, he wrote, "the light has gone out of my life." He did not include mention of his first wife in his autobiography, and rarely spoke of her, not because he did not grieve, but because he was a man better able to handle physical demands than emotional ones. In the Dakota Territory, he turned to cattle ranching, riding Western style, and working as a deputy sheriff. One of his lifelong friends was Seth Bullock, who may be better known to contemporary television viewers as one of the characters in the acclaimed HBO series *Deadwood*.

Out West, he began to display some of the characteristics which would personify his public life in years to come. His efforts to organize ranchers to deal with overgrazing issues led to the creation of the Little Missouri Stockmen's Association. He also exhibited an interest in preserving the natural world, forming the Boone and Crockett Club, whose mission was to conserve big game animals and their habitats.

When he returned to the orderly East after his time in the Wild West two years later, he resumed the life of a Roosevelt. He married a childhood friend, Edith Kermit Carow and returned to his political interests. The organized, efficient Edith was a successful foil to her impulsive, rambunctious husband whose interests would take him from New York to Cuba to, in time, the White House.

Theodore Roosevelt Gets Noticed

He became New York City police commissioner, not a

position for an honest man, as the New York Police Department was renowned for its corruption. That reputation was destined to end. During the two years of his tenure, he appointed 1600 recruits based on their qualifications and not their political loyalties; he implemented physical exams; ordered the inspection of firearms, and had telephones installed in police stations. His work with the police brought him into contact with the unsavory elements of the city, but he didn't back away from the poverty. He met with reforming reporter Jacob Riis, whose book *How the Other Half Lives* was a shocking revelation to the city's well-heeled residents. TR didn't succumb to the power of the party to which he belonged or to the privileges of his class, and Riis praised Roosevelt for his work.

Roosevelt moved into national office when he was made President William McKinley's Assistant Secretary of the Navy. He had Cuba firmly in his sights, believing that the Spanish presence on the island was a violation of the Monroe Doctrine. When the explosion of the American battleship Maine took place in the harbor of Havana and the Secretary of the Navy was called out of the office, Roosevelt capitalized upon his absence with the four hours he'd been given as acting Secretary. During that time, he prepared for war by ordering supplies, ammunition, and asking Congress for the authority to recruit sailors for the battle to come.

When the Spanish-American War inflamed American outrage and the nation's media in 1898, Roosevelt saw his chance for military action. He formed a volunteer cavalry unit that would achieve renown for his charge up San Juan Hill. The Rough Riders were volunteers from Oklahoma, Texas, New Mexico and Arizona, chosen from that region because the climate was similar to that of Cuba. The unit was comprised of what may be one of the motliest groups of fighting men in American history: Ivy League athletes, Texas Rangers, Native Americans, ranchers, miners, and glee club singers. The actual commander of the unit was Colonel Leonard Ward, but with Teddy Roosevelt as second-in-command, the Rough Riders were destined to attract attention. When Wood was placed in command of a cavalry brigade, the unit then became known as Roosevelt's Rough Riders.

Roosevelt and the soldiers received training and thanks to Roosevelt's connections, they were well equipped. Their uniforms were uniquely their own, however: trousers, shirt, leggings, boots, a slouch hat and handkerchiefs that were knotted loosely around their necks.

He preferred being addressed as "colonel" after his dramatic war exploits. The war hero returned home with a reputation that got him elected New York's governor the same year. As governor, he espoused ideas that were not shared by the political bosses of New York; Roosevelt's focus on honesty and responsibility, and putting the needs of New York and its people ahead of personal interests were bound to clash with the ruling self-interest of the movers and shakers behind the scenes.

Roosevelt governed in a time of manifest corruption and his integrity made enemies. TR was living in an era when self-interest was virtually sanctioned by the political machinery of the city, which meant that his reformer policies only aggravated the Republican Party bosses. Searching for a way to get rid of him and at the same time nullify him, they managed to have him made vice president to William McKinley, the Republican presidential candidate in the election of 1900. It seemed like the perfect solution. Vice Presidents were invisible.

But fate foiled the political bosses. On September 6, 1901, at the Pan American Exposition, an anarchist who had lost his job shot President McKinley. Anarchy was the terrorism of its day, responsible for numerous bombings and assassinations throughout Europe, killing monarchs and elected leaders alike. Presidential security was in its infancy, despite the fact that the country had already lost two presidents, Abraham Lincoln and James Garfield, within a relatively short time. McKinley disliked the encumbrances of security, feeling that they separated him from connecting to the people. Leon Czolgosz, who viewed McKinley as a symbol of oppression, shot McKinley twice. By the next day, Theodore Roosevelt had assumed the office of President of the United States. The invisible vice president was suddenly thrust into the national spotlight.

Roosevelt Takes the Stage

A young and vigorous president with a young and growing family caught the public's attention. The Roosevelt brood—Theodore III, Kermit, Ethel, Archibald, Quentin—along with Alice from his first marriage—enjoyed the attention of newspaper reporters. The Roosevelt brood included the entourage one might expect of a large family: dogs, birds, and a pony. For the children, the White House was a fascinating place to explore. Like their father, they were lively and curious. They roller-skated and rode their bicycles on the hardwood floors; they ascended the stairs on wooden stilts; they played on the furniture, and wreaked family havoc on the stately White House. The entire family enjoyed horseback riding, and the pony traveled via the elevator to the children's bedrooms from the basement.

Lunches were shared with guests and the Roosevelt's social network must have challenged the White House staff because the table size often had to be increased to accommodate the extra places. The guests were not confined to politics; one visitor was a champion wrestler who wrestled with the president and coached the Roosevelt children on techniques. They were as intellectual as they were active. The children shared their father's passion for reading, and Roosevelt might finish several books in one evening.

They were a lively family, and daughter Alice was particularly adventurous and outspoken. Her father once said of Alice, "I can either run the country or I can attend to Alice, but I cannot possibly do both."

As First Lady, Edith Roosevelt oversaw the renovation of the White House and took an active role in the social scene of Washington D.C. While his wife attended to the domestic matters, Roosevelt was as vigorous in his reforming as president as he had been in his prior role as governor, holding to his slogan to give people a "Square Deal." In a time when regulation was limited, Roosevelt supported legislation that required foods and pharmaceuticals to meet established standards. He became known as the Trust Buster because of his determination to break up the influential corporations like Standard Oil, and reduce their power. He pursued his passion for conservation to provide government protection to the nation's forests and parks, and named the first national monument, Devils Tower in Wyoming after signing the Antiquities Act. In 1906, the American president received the Nobel Peace Prize for his role in ending the war between Russia and Japan.

He championed the construction of the Panama Canal so that ships could travel a shorter route from the Atlantic to the Pacific Ocean, rather than having to navigate Cape Horn, which was perilous. Europeans had wanted a canal in Central America as far back as the 16th century and as trade with the Western Hemisphere increased, the economic desirability of a shorter travel route became obvious. In 1882, a French company had begun working on a canal that would cross the Colombian Isthmus of Panama to unite the Pacific and Atlantic Oceans. The endeavor saw thousands die, $287 million spent, slow progress and then, in 1888, the company failed.

Upon becoming president, Roosevelt had told Congress that nothing that could be undertaken on the continent was of as much consequence to the American people as the building of the Panama Canal. The next year the United States made a deal to buy the rights to the French equipment and property for no more than $40 million. The next step was to reach an agreement with Colombia, but Colombia was not amenable. The solution was a contrived revolution arranged by Roosevelt and Panamanian business interests to separate Panama from Colombia. The Americans had written a constitution for Panama in advance of the separation; a pro-canal lobbyist's wife had sewn a flag for the expediently created country.

Digging resumed, but in the beginning, the American effort was no more successful than what the French had accomplished. Disease struck, food spoiled, money flowed with nothing to show for it, and living conditions were discouraging. Then a new engineer arrived. John Stevens had built the Great Northern Railroad across the Pacific Northwest, and he was experienced with rough terrain. Realizing that what was needed was a healthy work force, Stevens began with sanitation to clean the work area, draining swamps, paving roads, spraying pesticides, and installing plumbing. Teddy Roosevelt was no longer president when the work was finally concluded and the Panama Canal opened on August 15, 1914. The Panama Canal, an indication of American technological innovation and economic might, was a major, was regarded as one of the most important building projects of the era. It was in so many ways typical of Teddy Roosevelt, who when he was determined, was unstoppable.

When Roosevelt's term ended in 1909 and the family moved out of the White House, the former president commented "I don't think any family has enjoyed the White House more than we have." When he left office, he believed that his successor and friend, William Howard Taft, would continue his policies, but disappointment with Taft's conservative direction led Roosevelt to form a third party in an attempt for a third presidential term. The Progressive or Bull Moose Party was built upon reform and included giving women the right to vote, the direct election of U.S. senators, and reduction of tariffs. Social worker Jane Addams spoke at the convention that nominated Roosevelt. Roosevelt's progressive credentials were already well known and he campaigned on the theme of a "Square Deal," which supported fair business competition and more social aid for Americans who were needy.

He was campaigning in Milwaukee when he was shot by an anarchist who stated that any presidential candidate seeking a third term deserved to be shot. Roosevelt, who probably would have been a media darling had he been a candidate for office in today's media-driven coverage, immediately turned the attack into a campaign bonus, announcing that it would take more than a gunshot to kill a Bull Moose. But with the split among the Republicans, Democrat Woodrow Wilson won the election.

Roosevelt didn't languish after the lost election. He decided to go on a speaking tour of Brazil and Argentina and take a cruise of the Amazon River. But then the government of Brazil invited him to accompany Brazilian explorer Candido Rondon, who was exploring the River of Doubt; the river had been previously unknown and its headwaters had just been discovered. The appeal of an adventure was all that Roosevelt needed. Edith Roosevelt was not so enthusiastic; she persuaded their son Kermit, who had just gotten engaged, to accompany his father and look out for him. The expedition faced disease from the insects, festering wounds, unsuitable canoes which were often lost in the rapids, poorly chosen provisions, and hostile natives. Roosevelt had a wound that became infected. Fortunately for the beleaguered expedition, seringueiros or rubber men who earned a living tapping rubber from rubber trees to provide tires for automobiles in the United States, came to their aid. Roosevelt made it home again, but his health was impaired by the events of the trip.

Theodore Roosevelt died seven years after his last election. His widow, Edith, outlived him, dying in 1919 and continuing an active interest in Republican politics until her death. The political split between the Roosevelts would become noteworthy when Franklin Delano Roosevelt ran for president in 1932 but did not receive the endorsement of TR's widow.

Why was Theodore Roosevelt Important?

The character and exploits of Teddy Roosevelt have defined him as America's first modern president. He also expanded the office of the president, following the example of fellow Republican Abraham Lincoln in the previous century. The eighteenth century had seen Congress dominate American governance, but under Roosevelt, the president became the center of the American political system. Like Lincoln, Roosevelt felt that he had an obligation to the country and to the electorate, and believed that the president was to serve as an agent of reform to support the public and improve their lives. Roosevelt was as pragmatic as he was idealistic: if the Constitution did not specifically deny a presidential power, Roosevelt interpreted this as something the president was authorized to use. Under Roosevelt, the progressive movement gained credibility, and instead of merely being the hobbyhorse of reformers, agitators, advocates and media personalities, it was stamped with the White House seal of approval.

No isolationist, Roosevelt promoted American involvement in international affairs. Simultaneously, he strengthened America's naval power, believing that the Navy would be vital in preventing enemies from attacking the United States.

Modern-day Americans are used to the role that image plays in national elections. Roosevelt's personal appeal for voters changed the isolated role that campaigns had formerly adopted. Voters who put him into office did not see him as a Republican, they saw him as Teddy Roosevelt. He was comfortable with the media and used them as well to advance his political aims by influencing public opinion. His enthusiasm was something new in the political arena, but Theodore Roosevelt governed as he lived, never holding back.

Teddy Roosevelt consistently ranks high when compared to other presidents. One of the reasons, although it's seldom mentioned, is the fact that he was able to guide the nation to a prosperous and stable time despite the unrest following the assassination of his predecessor, President William McKinley. As a symbol of American vigor and resourcefulness, Roosevelt imprinted his country on the century that would later be known as "The American Century." He was able to expand America's role in the world by increasing his nation's influence and power. He was a modern president for a new century.

The only 20th century president to accompany Washington, Jefferson, and Lincoln upon Mount Rushmore, Theodore Roosevelt would likely have succeeded in any endeavor, even if he had never taken his place upon the American political stage. He was a naturalist, a writer, a soldier, an adventurer, a reformer, a conservationist, a diplomat, a scholar, a husband and a father. He was a quintessential American whose innate talents defied stereotypes. He believed in the ability of a man to define his own destiny; he experienced great tragedy in his life and countered it with the rugged individualism that showed how a man, as well as a country, could be a frontier that needed the right kind of taming to make peace with life's wildness. In a modern perspective, his role as a pioneer environmentalist marks him as unique; he enjoyed the hunt while believing that the habitats of animals deserved to be preserved. In many ways he was both an idealist and a pragmatist, but he remains one of the Republican Party's most exemplary presidents, perhaps because he successfully embodied both idealism and pragmatism in his presidency.

Chapter 6 - Franklin Delano Roosevelt: The President Who Triumphed Over Adversity

Who was Franklin Delano Roosevelt?

There were, in truth, two Franklin Delano Roosevelts. The first Franklin Delano Roosevelt was handsome, debonair, and privileged, born to wealth and social status, doted on by his mother, who remained an integral part of his life even after he married his cousin Eleanor Roosevelt. Success came easily to him. Although he was a Democrat and his distant cousin, President Theodore Roosevelt a Republican, the two shared progressive leanings and a concern for the public welfare that was not always displayed by others of their class. Those who knew him expected him to achieve great things. Until he was stricken with polio in 1921. It was polio, when he was 39 years old that transformed him into the second FDR, paralyzed from the waist down and dependent upon a wheelchair, who had to struggle merely to move one foot in front of the other. The man who had lived a life of entitlement could no longer walk without assistance from others. What he could not physically do transformed him into a man who was willing to confront adversity, whether it was paralysis of his body or paralysis of a nation struck by a depression, to bring about hope. No longer entitled, he recognized that other people had their own "polio" to overcome whether it was economic distress, social discrimination, or lack of education. The disease that closed his physical independence opened up his compassion, giving him the ability to serve as president when fear and failure threatened to overcome the American public.

In the Beginning

There were two branches of the New York Roosevelts, the Hyde Park clan, to which Franklin was born in 1882, and the Oyster Bay Roosevelts, the family of Theodore Roosevelt. Both families were notable in their home stage of New York, but the Hyde Park branch was Democrat, the Oyster Bay branch Republican. Franklin's father James was 52 when his only child was born; wife Sara Delano was much younger. Living a life of privilege in the Gilded Age meant the best schools, trips to Europe, with tennis, polo, and sailing for sports. FDR followed the expected route; in education, first Groton then Harvard, passing the New York State Bar exam, a job on Wall street with a prestigious legal firm, followed by marriage to his orphaned cousin, Eleanor, President Roosevelt's favorite niece, who gave away the bride at their wedding in 1905.

Franklin Roosevelt the Husband

Unlike her husband, Anna Eleanor Roosevelt had not grown up as the adored child. Her mother was beautiful, her father an alcoholic. Her mother called her "Granny" because the child was so sober and old-fashioned in her behavior. In 1892, Anna Hall Roosevelt died of diphtheria; her younger brother Elliott, Jr. died the same year. Eleanor's father Elliot died in 1894 when he jumped from a window of the sanitarium where he had been confined because of his alcoholism. After the death of her parents, Eleanor was raised by her grandmother and at 15, she went abroad to study in London, where she learned to speak French fluently. She left the school reluctantly in 1902 so that she could accede to her grandmother's wish to make her debut in society.

Later that year, Eleanor and her fifth cousin, Franklin, began a secret romance and became engaged in 1903. Sara Delano Roosevelt, who had a great deal of influence over her son, tried to discourage the romance but Roosevelt was adamant. Even a Caribbean cruise in 1904 failed to steer Roosevelt away from his marital intentions.

Eleanor as a young bride had little power in the household; the Roosevelt home was provided by her mother-in-law and connected to Sara's home through sliding doors. Sara's influence extended to the children that Eleanor bore. Eleanor gave birth to six children within ten years; the first son named Franklin died in infancy. But Sara was a dominant force in their upbringing.

The Roosevelts had been married for 13 years when Eleanor found love letters written by her social secretary, Lucy Mercer, to her husband, who considered leaving his wife for his mistress. Roosevelt's infidelity distressed his awkward, shy wife, but while Sara Delano had not been an advocate of Eleanor as a daughter-in-law, she was not tolerant of her son's marital misadventures and told him that, if he divorced his wife, she would disinherit him. Roosevelt, aware of the effect that a divorce would have on his political future, elected to stay with his wife, but his infidelity forever changed the dynamic of their marriage. But as the romantic nature of their marriage diminished, their political partnership was destined to grow.

Franklin Roosevelt Gets Noticed

Politics must have seemed like a family legacy. Franklin Roosevelt won a seat in the state senate in 1910. Like his cousin, he ran afoul of the party bosses, in his case the Tammany Hall Democrats, who pulled the strings behind the scenes. He supported the candidacy of Woodrow Wilson for president in 1912, and when Wilson won, Roosevelt was named Assistant Secretary of the Navy. He espoused aviation, submarines, and innovation, running into obstacles from those who scoffed at such modern ideas. During his time in the position, he learned to negotiate with Congress to get things done, as well as gaining a background in dealing with labor; when the United States entered World War I, he was introduced to the role that government played in outfitting the military. After the Democratic Party lost the 1920 election with Roosevelt as the vice presidential candidate, the Roosevelts left Washington D.C. to return to New York.

Franklin Roosevelt Takes the Stage

In 1921, Roosevelt fell overboard while sailing on his yacht. The next day, he went for a swim to alleviate back pain, but as the day went on, his legs became weaker. By the third day, he could no longer bear his own weight. Eleanor contacted doctors for answers but their diagnoses couldn't seem to identify the problem. Then a doctor diagnosed infantile paralysis, known as polio. He told Roosevelt to take hot baths rather than having massages, which could have been making the condition worse. It was uncommon for an adult of Roosevelt's age to contract the disease. No one could figure out when he'd actually contracted the virus, but it's possible that he contracted it at a Boy Scout camp in New York before heading to the family cottage at Campobello Island.

When polio left him without the use of his legs, it looked as though Franklin Roosevelt would have to redefine his destiny. He spent several years concentrating on overcoming his paralysis, swimming three times a week. By winter, he had built up the strength in his arms, his stomach and lower back were strong, and his nervous system was functioning normally. In 1922, he was fitted with brackets and by spring, he was able to stand up with help. He lived out of the limelight for a time while he physically adapted to his altered state of health. He exercised at every opportunity with the goal of one day being able to walk. He refused to allow negativity to interfere with his efforts and he insisted that people in his company maintained a cheerful demeanor.

In 1924, he began to visit Warm Springs Georgia in the hopes that the waters would cure him. That didn't happen, but his visits became regular. When financial problems struck Warm Springs, Roosevelt bought the facility and turned it into a rehabilitation center for polio patients.

Roosevelt was uncomfortable in the cumbersome wheelchairs that were available, so he designed one that suited his purposes. He replaced the legs of a dining room chair with bicycle-like wheels. Small and mobile, able to access narrow hallways and tight corners, his wheelchair did not call attention to his condition because of its resemblance to a familiar piece of household furniture. He fully intended to return to political life, and mindful of his image, he avoided being photographed in his wheelchair. He wore iron braces on his legs and used a cane so that he seemed to be able to walk, albeit for very short distances. Attitudes toward the disabled were not likely to inspired confidence, especially for a man who sought political advancement. But instead of shunning him, the public welcomed him, regarding his condition with sympathy. Encouraged by the public response, Roosevelt resumed his political career.

In 1928, he ran for governor and squeaked out a win.

He concentrated on social reform and won a second term, this time by a respectable margin. As the Great Depression deepened and it was obvious that Herbert Hoover would be a one-term president, the Democrats made connections with labor, minorities and Southern white voters to build a base of the electorate who had faith that FDR's "New Deal" would bring back prosperity. He was the winning candidate in 42 of the 48 states, transforming the Democratic Party into the political voice for diverse segments of the population and organized labor.

March 4, 1933, when he was inaugurated, was the year when the Depression was at its worst. Manufacturing centers were demoralized by the lack of jobs; unemployment in 1933 was 80 percent in Toledo, Ohio and even worse, almost 90 percent, in Lowell, Massachusetts. In his first inaugural address, FDR declared, "The only thing we have to fear is fear itself." But for a nation suffering, on average, 25 percent unemployment, a 50% drop in industrial production and plummeting farm prices, the fear was very real. The day after his inauguration, he issued a bank holiday to prevent people from withdrawing their money. The Emergency Banking Act reorganized the banks, closing the insolvent ones. When he had his first fireside chat, he encouraged Americans to trust the banks and return their savings to their accounts. By the end of March, almost three-fourths of the banks were once again in operation.

FDR's first 100 days in office attacked the economic ills with relief programs designed to provide work and funding to lift the nation out of the Depression. More New Deal legislation would follow, including the Works Progress Administration, the Social Security Act, and the National Labor Relations Act. Congress ended Prohibition and once again, Americans could purchase alcohol. The Tennessee Valley Authority Act gave the government the power to build dams along the Tennessee River so that flooding could be controlled and affordable hydroelectric power could be generated. Farmers of corn, wheat, dairy products and tobacco were paid to let their fields remain fallow so that surpluses would end and prices would rise.

Franklin Roosevelt may have lacked mobility, but the First Lady was known as her husband's eyes and ears, able to go where he could not. His election revitalized Eleanor Roosevelt's role in the marriage. She had been the one who, when he was stricken by polio, encouraged him to continue his political career despite his mother's view that he should recognize his deficiencies and retire from public life. She was the first of the First Ladies to have press conferences for the media; she wrote a syndicated column for newspapers and even earned money giving speeches on the lecture circuit. She met with labor leaders, supported African-Americans in their quest for civil rights and welcomed them to the White House, and defended the loyalty of Japanese-Americans who were interned during World War II. She became a target for her visibility at a time when women were still expected to adopt a recessive role in deference to their husbands, but her willingness to meet with constituents served FDR's political needs. Eleanor Roosevelt had become her own woman and was no longer in the shadow of either her husband or her mother-in-law.

The nation's recovery took time, but voters had confidence in FDR, re-electing him in 1936. By the election of 1940, Europe was at war with Nazi Germany, but Americans wanted no part of foreign entanglements. Nonetheless, FDR opened up a dialogue with Winston Churchill, who became prime minister of Great Britain in 1940. FDR realized that while the nation was not reconciled to the notion of war, American neutrality would be short-lived.

"December 7, a day which will live in infamy," was

Roosevelt's declaration of war before Congress after the Japanese attacked Pearl Harbor. In the course of an attack that lasted for two hours, the Japanese sank or damaged 18 warships and destroyed 164 aircraft. Over 2400 servicemen and civilians were killed. American went from isolationist neutrality to a state of war. Roosevelt, Churchill, and Joseph Stalin of the Soviet Union formed an alliance against the Axis Powers of Germany, Italy, and Japan. The United States mobilized quickly, and the home front joined the war effort with vigor.

The country was not prepared for a war on this scale on the European and the Pacific fronts. Industry switched to wartime production, new factories were built, and the government was required to spend at unprecedented rates. Roosevelt had instituted a peacetime draft in 1940 and by December of 1941 the military had grown to 2.2 million. The draft brought in 10 million.

On the home front, the Depression was over as the war effort meant that unemployment vanished. The Gross National Product went from $99.7 billion in 1940 to almost $212 billion by 1945. In 1940, Roosevelt had told Congress that he wanted the country to construct 50,000 aircraft per year. By 1944, America was building nearly twice that many.

Because of the labor shortage, women entered the workforce, earning higher wages by working in defense plants. When a protest was threatened because African Americans and minorities were discriminated against in defense factories, Roosevelt acted, creating the Fair Employment Practices Commission to investigate the charges of unfair practices against minority workers.

The country was changing, not only because of the war but because of the leadership of a dynamic president who believed that obstacles could be overcome. But the years were taking their toll. FDR was re-elected in 1944, although by this time his health was in serious decline. He was the only president to run for and be elected to four terms in office. The war was going well and it was apparent that the Allies were going to win. The victorious, although costly, invasion of Normandy in June of 1944 did not instantly defeat the Germans, but it was clear that the Third Reich was in its final days. The war against Japan had begun to look more promising after the naval victory at Midway, but the Japanese were determined not to surrender and the war stretched on.

FDR's doctors had ordered him to rest because of his health, but a wartime president has little down time. He was at Warm Springs, Georgia on March 29, 1945, when he fell unconscious and died later the same day; his doctor ruled the cause of death as a massive cerebral hemorrhage. A month later, the nation celebrated victory over Germany on V-E Day. His vice president, Harry Truman, had not been privy to the information about the top-secret Manhattan Project, but was soon let in on the secret of a terrible new weapon. On August 6, 1945 Truman finished what FDR had begun when he ordered the dropping of the atomic bomb on Hiroshima. When a second bomb was dropped on Nagasaki three days later, Japan was devastated. Japan surrendered on August 15, bringing World War II to an end.

Why was Franklin Roosevelt Important?

A two-term president, which is now as many terms a president is constitutionally allow to serve, would not have had to deal with all the issues that FDR in his four terms had to face: the Great Depression; labor unrest; the rise of militarism across the world; World War II; the volatile alliance with America's former and future foe, the communist Soviet Union; the rise of civil rights; the changing social canvas of the country and the transformation of America into a world power. But in order to understand the role that Franklin Roosevelt played, one needs to revisit the state of the world at the time he achieved his goal of becoming president. From the giddy recklessness of the roaring 20s had come the crash of the stock market in 1929. People were desperate and looking for someone to blame. In 1933, an Austrian painter named Adolf Hitler was appointed chancellor of Germany after his Nazi Party won seats in the 1932 election. The German people, devastated by the crippling reparations imposed upon them by the triumphant European powers at the treaty of Versailles, needed a savior, and Hitler assumed the role. He nourished them on the myth of Aryan superiority and sent six million Jews to their death to pay the price for Germany's prior suffering.

But in 1933, when Franklin Delano Roosevelt took office as the country reeled from 25 percent unemployment and a paralyzed economy, he rallied the Americans with hope, not with military posturing. The nation was far from exempt from its own bigotry, as African-Americans, Jews, and Catholics were victimized. But the nation did not vote its fears, it voted its hopes. Those hopes were personified by a handicapped man in a wheelchair who could not stand without the support of what he jocularly referred to as "ten pounds of steel" bracing his legs. FDR led his nation in war not to subjugate other nations or to oppress them, but to free Americans and the world from the dark threat of Nazism, fascism, and militarism. Hope, rather than fear, triumphed.

Chapter 7 - Martin Luther King, Jr: The Man with a Dream

Who was Martin Luther King, Jr.?

For young people in the United States, segregated schools, buses, lunch counters and bathrooms are stories in history books. They believe that it happened, but it's so foreign to their understanding of how people should be treated that they can be forgiven for not comprehending how racism had been a way of life for most of the centuries that America has been a nation. That racism, Jim Crow laws, and segregation came to an end is due to the courage of many black men and women who boycotted buses, endured beatings, and faced death threats but kept the faith and believed in the dream that one day, they would be acknowledged as equals in the land where freedom was regarded as a birthright. The man who made the dream a reality was a Baptist minister who envisioned an America in which men and women would be judged not by the color of their skin but by the content of their character. He predicted that he might not reach that Promised Land with them, and he was right; an assassin's bullet ended the life of Martin Luther King, Jr. but the dream could not be killed.

In the Beginning

Jim Crow laws in the South kept "separate but equal" status a way of life for African-Americans. Under Jim Crow, the barriers separating blacks and whites were codified and enforced: segregation affected buses and trains; schools, parks and libraries; restrooms and restaurants. There was no subtlety in the process: signs indicating "Colored" guaranteed that African-Americans knew their place. The laws were based on the "separate but equal" policy which had been authorized by the 1896 Supreme Court decision Plessy v. Ferguson. For decades, no one had challenged the practice, but those days were about to come to an end.

Martin Luther King's grandfather and father were Baptist ministers, but the family came from sharecropper stock. He was born on January 15, 1929 in Atlanta. His father, Michael King, Sr., changed his name to Martin Luther King, Sr. in honor of the leader of the 16th century Protestant Reformation, Martin Luther, whose revolutionary ideas about religion, faith, and how men answered to God toppled the world order. No one was saying that the pastor of the Ebenezer Baptist Church was on a par with Martin Luther, but in time, his son would also change his name and the world order would also be altered as a result of his actions in the name of God.

The Kings grew up in a South where racism was a way of life, but in the King household, the children were taught that all God's children were equal, black and white alike. At Booker T. Washington High School, young King was smart enough to skip two grades, but when he became a freshman at Morehouse College at the age of 15, he seemed adrift. His doubts about religion, hardly atypical in a teenager, were an affront to his father, who regarded the ministry as the obvious career for his oldest son. Ultimately, however, he returned to the fold of the faithful and after receiving his degree in sociology, he became a student at Crozer Theological Seminary, where he was elected student body president and was class valedictorian. However, he displeased his straight-laced father with his leisure activities which included drinking and sexual involvement with a white woman.

King the Husband

While studying for his PhD, he met a student at the New England Conservatory School in Boston, Massachusetts; Coretta Scott had been awarded a fellowship to the school after receiving her Bachelor of Arts degree in music and education from Antioch College in Ohio. Scott's family was committed to obtaining an education for their children, and she had been the valedictorian of her high school graduating class. She earned a second degree in voice in violin, but she found time for the theology student at Boston University.

In 1953, King married Coretta Scott. The pair would become the parents of four children who, because they were the offspring of the civil rights activists, grew up surrounded by the movement, but also aware of the threats that activism posed. The couple traveled on behalf of their causes, but even when they traveled internationally to places such as Mexico, India, and Ghana, they were on a mission to learn more about the plight of others.

King Gets Noticed

By the age of 25, King had earned his doctorate and was the pastor of the Dexter Avenue Baptist Church in Montgomery, Alabama. It would not be long before

Montgomery's bigotry and King's convictions would collide.

The rule on public transportation in Montgomery was that black-skinned commuters were relegated to the back of the bus. On December 1, 1955, Rosa Parks, an African-American seamstress, was seated in the front row of what was designated as the colored section. As the bus filled up and seats were occupied, the bus driver ordered Parks and other black riders to relinquish their seats so that the white passengers who were standing could be seated. Parks refused. She was arrested for violating the Montgomery City Code. When local civil rights leaders learned what had happened, they planned a bus boycott, with the young pastor the Rev. Dr. Martin Luther King, Jr. as its leader. For over a year, black workers walked to work, boycotting the buses that denied them their rights. King's home was attacked, and for Montgomery's African-Americans, it was a time of violence and threats. But finally, Montgomery surrendered; public transportation was no longer segregated by skin color.

The 1950s were coming to an end, and a new era was dawning. The formation of the Southern Christian Leadership Conference in 1957 was a foundation for civil rights activists like King to challenge the policies of

116

the South which made blacks second-class citizens. They resolved to use non-violent protests to make their case; a visit to India, the homeland of Mohandas Gandhi, the leader who had used civil disobedience to win his country's independence, inspired King to adopt peaceful protest in his own crusade. Black men and women engaged in sit-ins, where they would set at segregated lunch counters. They were insulted and sometimes physically abused, but the sit-ins were successful. Like the buses, lunch counters were learning that the peaceful protests were changing the way they did business.

King Takes the Stage

King and his family moved back to Atlanta in 1960 where he shared the responsibilities of pastoring the Ebenezer Baptist Church with his father. By now his civil rights work was no longer a local event. When he was imprisoned for violating his probation for a traffic violation, his wife received a telephone call from Democratic presidential candidate John F. Kennedy, who expressed his sympathy for her plight and offered his help if it was needed. Three years later, King was again jailed, this time in Birmingham, Alabama, where the police set their dogs on civil rights demonstrators.

King's book, *Letters from Birmingham Jail* became a

sort of manifesto of the civil rights movement. The protestors used the tactics of civil disobedience and nonviolence, but the response was often violent and uncivil. In his book, he wrote, "I cannot sit idly by in Atlanta and not be concerned about what happens in Birmingham. Injustice anywhere is a threat to justice everywhere. . . . Whatever affects one directly, affects all indirectly."

Nonviolence was not an easy option, but King believed that resisting the temptation to use violence forced communities to negotiate and deal with the issue.

By 1963, King was attracting national attention and the Federal Bureau of Investigation was monitoring his activities. FBI Director J. Edgar Hoover had obtained the permission of Attorney General Robert Kennedy, the president's brother, to monitor King's private life. The FBI hoped to prove that the civil rights activist was working with communists. That evidence never materialized. But their surveillance, which included bugging his hotel rooms, revealed that King was unfaithful to his wife when he was traveling. Coretta King was aware of her husband's unfaithfulness, and the FBI made sure that she knew when they sent a tape of his sexual philandering to her home. According to Ralph Abernathy, King's close associate, they all, including King, realized that adultery was wrong. King, Abernathy wrote, "had a particularly difficult time with that temptation."

To the FBI, King was a threat to national security. But to millions of Americans, black and white, King was the leader who would conquer the evils of bigotry and racism and help the country overcome the prejudice which the United States needed to overcome if all Americans could truly be free. In August, 1963, King's March on Washington drew 200,000 marchers, black and white, men and women, individuals and organizations, lay people and clergy. King's "I Have a Dream" speech became a clarion call for civil rights for black Americans who had been liberated by the Civil War but had not been allowed to enjoy the full harvest of freedom. King's speech is regarded as one of the greatest speeches of the 20th century. "I have a dream that one day this nation will rise up and live out the true meaning of its creed: 'We hold these truths to be self-evident: that all men are created equal.' I have a dream that one day on the red hills of Georgia the sons of former slaves and the sons of former slave owners will be able to sit down together at a table of brotherhood."

In 1964, the Civil Rights Act was passed, which meant

that discrimination was a violation of federal law. King was awarded the Nobel Peace Prize that year for his work, but an international prize and a national law didn't change the fact that for many in the South, King was a troublemaker who needed to be stopped if the traditional way of life was to be maintained.

Discrimination was officially forbidden thanks to the Civil Rights Act, but efforts by the Southern Christian Leadership Council (SNLC) and the Student Nonviolent Coordinating Committee (SNIC) to register blacks to vote were fiercely resisted by white who were unwilling to share political power. The statistics were daunting: in Selma, Alabama, only two percent of black voters, or 300 people, were registered to vote out of 15,000 eligible black voters. King decided that Selma would be the focus of a campaign to register black voters. Led by segregationist Governor George Wallace, white supremacists in Selma were determined to block the efforts. When a young African-American was killed by a state trooper, King and SNIC planned a protest march that would begin in Selma and end in Montgomery, 54 miles away. When the 600 marchers reached the Edmund Pettis Bridge, Alabama police officers with tear gas, whips, and nightsticks halted their progress and beat them back to Selma. Watching on television, a nation was horrified by the violent spectacle.

Several days later, King was present as the marchers tried to cross the Edmond Pettus Bridge, where state police barricades waited. King and his followers knelt in prayer, and turned back, unable to cross the bridge. Governor Wallace and Alabama state officials continued to try to block the march, but they were ordered by a U.S. district court judge to allow the march to proceed. Speaking on national television, President Lyndon Johnson vowed to lobby for passage of new voting rights legislation he planned to introduce. When the marchers set out from Selma on March 21, 1965, their entourage included the Alabama National Guard and federal troops. The marchers, walking 12 hours a day, reached Montgomery on March 25. Upon their arrival at the state capitol, they were met by 50,000 supporters.

In August, Congress passed the Voting Rights Act, which banned literacy tests as a voting requirement, mandated federal oversight of the voter registration process in areas where voting tests had formerly been used, and authorized the U.S. Attorney General to challenge the use of poll taxes in state and local elections.

King's status had passed national boundaries and he was recognized all over the world as the civil rights leader who was striving to bring equality to a race that had been oppressed for far too long. Young black leaders, impatient at the slow pace of progress, felt that nonviolence was a weak way to espouse their just cause and they criticized King's leadership as passive. Activists like Malcolm X spoke out against King's policy of nonviolence because they felt the oppression of blacks by the whites in power kept African-Americans in subjugation.

King was burdened by the heavy load of his leadership and by the friction with other groups, but he saw that the movement was making progress. However, King had begun to realize that civil rights was not merely an issue of race. In an era of protest, King saw connections linking racial discrimination, economic poverty and the unpopular war in Viet Nam. His goal was to form a coalition made up of poor Americans, transcending race, to bring poverty and unemployment to the forefront of national attention. His protests broadened to include these issues which had the 1960s in turmoil.

The 1960s were a violent decade. John Kennedy was president for just three years when he was assassinated in 1963. Civil rights leaders such as Medgar Evers had been assassinated. Malcolm X was felled by assassination in 1965. Nonviolence seemed to pale in comparison to the rage which gripped the nation. In April, 1968, King was planning a march on Washington that would broaden the scope of the issues for which they demonstrated.

The broadening scope of his advocacy for others was affecting his health. He was not sleeping well, suffered from migraines headaches, and was concerned about the young African-Americans who didn't see his work as relevant. But that didn't bring his effort to a halt.

In April, King and other members of SCLC went to Memphis, Tennessee to give support to a strike by sanitation workers. When he spoke at the Mason Temple Church that night, his words were prophetic as he said, "I've seen the promised land. I may not get there with you. But I want you to know tonight, that we, as a people, will get to the Promised Land. . . . I'm not fearing any man. Mine eyes have seen the glory of the coming of the Lord." He also warned his followers, "We've got some difficult days ahead."

The next evening, he shaved and put on cologne in preparation for a soul-food dinner. Before leaving, he stepped out onto the balcony on the second floor of the motel where he and the others were staying. A rifle shot hit him in the neck and slammed him against the wall. He was rushed to a hospital, where he died.

Rioting broke out in cities all across the countries. Robert F. Kennedy, campaigning to be the Democratic candidate for the presidency, announced the death of the civil rights leader to an Indianapolis crowd, poor and mostly black, that waited to hear him. Kennedy had been advised against going; his police escort left him and he was unprotected on a night when angry and grieving African-Americans were rioting in rage. He gave a moving speech recognizing the attributes of King and the crowd went home in peace. Two months later, he himself was killed by an assassin's bullet. Violence, it seemed, had seized the era.

Three days after King's assassination, Congress passed the Civil Rights Act of 1968, also known as the Fair Housing Act.

Two months later, James Earl Ray was arrested at Heathrow Airport in London and named as the man who had killed King. His fingerprints were on the rifle that had killed King, and in 1969, Ray pleaded guilty to the charge of murder. No testimony was given in the trial and he was sentenced to 99 years imprisonment. In 1977, King's son Dexter met with Ray, who had recanted his confession. The King family wanted the case to be re-opened so that new information about the assassination could be presented. The King family felt that because he was building a coalition to force economic reforms and end the Viet Nam War, Martin Luther King was viewed as a threat. The Kings believed that the government had him assassinated because if his movement was successful, the ruling elite would be toppled. Ray died in 1998; the lingering questions regarding his role in the assassination never to be answered.

King's message did not die with him, His widow, Coretta Scott King, carried on after his death, traveling all over the world to meet with international leaders in support of the rights of women and children, the poor, the homeless, and other demographics which needed the support of a strong, credible voice. Although she had been the one to stay at home and raise the four children while her husband traveled on behalf of equal rights, she was a vocal advocate of the causes for which Martin Luther King lived and died. She founded the Martin Luther King, Jr. Center for Nonviolent Social Change in Atlanta, which welcomes more than a million visitors annually.

A national holiday recognizes his role in the nation's history as the states celebrate Martin Luther King Day in January. The establishment of a holiday in her husband's honor was one of the crusades to which his widow, Coretta Scott King, a civil rights activist in her own right, dedicated her efforts after her husband's death. In 1983, President Ronald Reagan signed the bill that made Martin Luther King Day a national holiday.

When he spoke in 1957 at the NAACP Emancipation Day Rally, King's words expressed his conviction that the quest for freedom demanded sacrifice. "I close by saying that there is nothing greater in all the world than freedom. It's worth going to jail for. It's worth losing a job for. It's worth dying for. My friends, go out this evening determined to achieve this freedom which God wants for all of his children."

Why was King Important?
Martin Luther King prophetically predicted that he would not reach the promised land of equality and equal rights to which he had dedicated his life. He suffered indignity, imprisonment, FBI surveillance and threats to his family. With his death, the civil rights movement had yet another martyr. But slowly, inexorably, attitudes changed. The laws passed in the 1960s created a new vision of America, one in which

the races were acknowledged as equal Americans. In 2009, when President Barack Obama took the oath of office, he and his wife and two daughters moved into the White House to live in a place where previously, people with dark skin were only servants. Without the struggles of the civil rights movement and the steadfast leadership of Martin Luther King, that landmark election might never have taken place.

Blacks who had been unseen in American political life and popular culture slowly began to take their place in America's living rooms after the civil rights movement's successes. African-Americans whose ancestors had known slavery became entrepreneurs and CEOs, astrophysicists and astronauts, football quarterbacks and models, politicians and presidents. It could be said that, until Martin Luther King embarked on his crusade for racial equality, the United States could not live up to the documents by which it lived, the ones that declared that all were created equal. Martin Luther King, Jr. made Thomas Jefferson's words come true.

Chapter 8 - Ronald Reagan: The Small-Town, Small-Government President

Who was Ronald Reagan?

He believed in the validity of the American dream because he had known hard times and poverty growing up, and because his Hollywood career made him trust in the power of the image of America, no matter how adverse the circumstances which the country faced. Ronald Wilson Reagan's ability to make the nation see his vision also saw him elected to two terms as president, as the conservative moment regained its momentum under his leadership. He supported American military might and leadership, believed in the ability of corporate strength to bring prosperity, and was convinced that smaller government was crucial for a stronger nation. During his presidency, his famous speech in Berlin at the Brandenburg Gate in 1987 was like a prophecy; his words, "Mr. Gorbachev, tear down this wall" seemed to herald the fall of the communist superpower, as two years later, the Berlin Wall came down and the land mass that was the Soviet Union became simply the Russian Federation. He was no longer in office when the Wall came down, but political observers credited his presidency with playing a strong role in the fall of communism. Knowing that Soviet tanks would not cross their borders imbued the East Germans with the courage to celebrate their freedom as pieces of the Berlin Wall all were chiseled away. Ronald Reagan entered the realm of legend with his presidency, but the real man was both ordinary and unique.

In the Beginning

Born in Illinois on February 6, 1911, Ronald Wilson Reagan was the child of parents who were frequently on the move. Reagan's father was an alcoholic and a failure at business, but the hardship of his early years did not dim Reagan's optimism or his belief in America's ability to make dreams come true. He was born in Tampico, Illinois, in an apartment his parents rented above a bakery/restaurant, across the street from where his father worked as a store clerk. Reagan, who would later charm the country with his folksy humor and lack of frills, described living in the White House as "living above the store" again. When they settled in Dixon, he settled too, into a successful life as a high school athlete, study body president, and actor.

He was good enough at sports to win a scholarship and at Illinois' Eureka College he played in three different sports: football, track and swimming. Again, he was elected president of the student council, and continued to act. His degrees were in economics and sociology but after graduation in 1932, jobs were hard to come by during the Great Depression, and Reagan found work as a sports announcer in radio.

Five years later, he was a Hollywood actor under contract with Warner Brothers. Over the course of his career, he acted in more than 50 films. Although he has been derided for the quality of his acting and his role as a "B" actor, he attracted favorable attention for his role in the film, *Knute Rockne, All American*, where he played the part of football hero George Gipp. Rockne's movie line, "Win one for the Gipper" would become part of Reagan's campaigning vocabulary when he left the world of acting for the political arena.

When World War II broke out, Reagan left acting to serve in the Army Air Force Motion Picture Unit. His poor eyesight had prevented him from serving in combat, and he spent the war years making training films for the Army, earning the rank of captain. The films were designed to inspire the nation with uplifting stories that evoked America's legacy of hope.

Reagan Gets Noticed

His political career was initiated by his role as president of the Screen Actors Guild during the time of the famous Holly wood blacklist, when the country and the entertainment industry feared the threat of communism. Reagan served as the SAG president for five consecutive terms from 1947-1952. The anti-communist fervor divided liberal and conservative elements of Hollywood; Reagan, who opposed communism, testified before the House Un-American Activities Committee, and provided the FBI with names of actors that he believed supported communist beliefs. His work in the zealous pursuit of communists among the acting community was a precursor to his efforts later in his political career to bring down the Soviets.

Reagan the Husband

In 1938, Ronald Reagan acted in the film *Brother Rat* with an actress named Jane Wyman; two years later, the couple married. They had two daughters, one who was born prematurely and died the same day, and adopted a son. The death of their child caused strains in the marriage. She filed for divorce in 1948, offering the explanation that it was due to a difference in politics; Wyman was a Republican and at the time,

Reagan was a Democrat. Although she did not offer salacious tidbits about her ex-husband when he became noteworthy in the political arena, her personal assistant confirmed that she voted for him in both the 1980 and 1984 elections.

In 1949, Reagan met Anne Frances Robbins, who had been signed by MGM Studios to a contract and re-named Nancy Davis. The young actress had been in Hollywood long enough to date Clark Gable, and long enough to unwittingly run afoul of the Hollywood blacklist. Reagan was the Screen Actors Guild president, and Nancy Davis was trying to have her name removed from the blacklist which counted her as a possible communist sympathizer. The mistake—the list actually referred to another actress with the same name---was keeping Davis from obtaining acting jobs, so she asked Reagan for help. They began dating, and in 1952, they were married. They worked together in the film *Hellcats of the Navy*, but then Davis left acting to care for their two children. Davis didn't regard the loss of her career as a sacrifice. She regarded marriage and motherhood to be the ultimate goal for a woman. "My life really began when I married my husband," she said. "A woman's real happiness and real fulfillment come from within the home with her husband and children."

Reagan Takes the Stage

He switched from motion pictures to television and as the host of General Electric Theater, he sometimes delivered 14 speeches in one day when he was touring GE plants. The work was very profitable and excellent training for a later time in life when his speeches would be heard by millions.

In 1962, Ronald Reagan switched from the Democratic Party to the Republican. His career as an actor was on the wane, but Reagan had found a new part to play in California politics. He was elected as governor in 1966 (when asked what kind of a governor he would be, the political novice joked that he didn't know because he'd never played a governor in his acting career), and reelected in 1970.

When the Reagans moved into the Governor's Mansion, they didn't last long. The fire department had described the mansion as a firetrap, and the Reagans moved to an exclusive suburb. The move was seen as evidence that the Reagans were snobs who were more concerned with living a wealthy lifestyle, an accusation which would resurface later in their political career.

California was a hotbed of the student protest

movement in the 1960s, and one of Reagan's campaign themes was to clean up the mess at Berkeley, referring to the University of California campus where antiwar and pro-civil rights protests were commonplace. Reagan said that his swearing-in took place at ten minutes after midnight because the outgoing Governor "Pat" Brown had been filling appointments in the waning days of his office. However, there was speculation that, because the time had been scheduled six weeks before the swearing-in, the decision might have been influenced by astrology.

Reagan had not speaking idly when targeted Berkeley as one of his campaign themes. He sent in the California Highway Patrol in 1969 to stop the protests; the episode was later called "Bloody Thursday." The National Guard occupied the city for two weeks to control the protesters.

He made his bid for national office several times, but was not named the candidate, as Richard Nixon won the Republican nomination and the White House in 1968, and Gerald Ford in 1976. He did achieve recognition on a national level, however, and was sent by President Nixon to represent the White House as a special envoy. During his two terms as governor, his political stance was established: smaller government, tax rebates, reducing dependence on welfare, anti-abortion, less government regulation. Although he signed a bill authorizing abortion, he later said that his inexperience had led to the signing and that he was actually pro-life rather than pro-choice. His political views would prove to be in synch with the electorate which was looking for a change after the Nixon Watergate scandal, the high inflation of the Ford presidency, and the perceived loss of American prestige and power under Jimmy Carter.

In 1980, the United States was disenchanted with incumbent President Jimmy Carter and his failure to bring the country out of what became known as its malaise. The Islamic revolution in Iran had taken Americans hostage; a rescue attempt had failed. For Americans in 1979, the overthrow of the Shah of Iran and his replacement with a government led by the Ayatollah Khomeini was an indication that American might had been dealt a severe blow. When Iranian students stormed the American embassy in Tehran and took 52 American diplomats and citizens hostages, the world realized that radical Islam, a new force in international politics, was beginning to be heard. Iran's distrust of the West and its determination to be governed by religious clerics would cast a long shadow over the Middle East for a long time to come. But no one realized that at the time.

Americans simply felt that it was time for a change. The country was looking for a dynamic leader who could make them believe in their destiny again. Ronald Reagan's candidacy was what they were looking for. For many Americans, however, Reagan's reputation did not inspire confidence. He was derided as a B actor whose Bonzo films did nothing to add to his acting luster. He was seen as a cowboy, someone whose political tactics owed more to the Old West than to established law. His right-wing views were seen as lacking in compassion. But for others, Reagan's promise that America's best days were still ahead and his description of the country as the shining on a hill validated their hope for their country's future.

Ronald Reagan became the 40th president of the United States, winning 489 electoral votes. He was the oldest person elected to the office of president, but he seemed youthful at the age of 69. He was also the first divorced man to be elected as president, but for the 1980 election, his previous marriage was not an issue. He was perceived as a man of action who would restore America's glory days.

What had been known as the Iran hostage crisis, which

saw 52 Americans held hostage by the Iranian government for 444 days, ended on the day of Reagan's inauguration. It was a sign for the American people that better days were in store.

Two months after Reagan's inauguration, John Hinckley, Jr. shot the president. Reagan famously told the first Lady, "Honey, I forgot to duck," exhibiting his low-key approach to what could have been a fatal shooting. Reagan was rushed into surgery and survived the attempt, although his press secretary, James Brady, suffered lasting injuries from his wounds. One of Reagan's first challenges as president came in August of the same year, when the air traffic controllers went on strike. When they refused his order to return to work, he fired more than 11,000 air traffic controllers and called in military air traffic controllers to work until new ones were trained. His decisive actions were not always popular, but they demonstrated a straightforward, no-nonsense approach to leadership that many Americans appreciated.

When Reagan took office, the United States was in the midst of rising inflation and unemployment. Reagan's economic solution, known as Reaganomics, focused on the reduction of the federal income tax and the capital gains tax, reduced government spending and regulation, and cutting inflation. He favored a return to free enterprise and supply-side economics rather than following the policies of economist John Maynard Keynes. The Economic Recovery Act of 1981 lowered tax rates, but even when tax rates in other areas increased, the recession which had lowered the nation's gross domestic product ended in 1982. Over the course of his two terms in office, the unemployment rate dropped significantly.

Not long after Reagan's inauguration, the First Lady turned her attention the White House renovation. The family quarters needed work, as the plaster was cracked, the paint was chipped, and the floors showed signs of wear. Nancy Reagan sought private donations to cover the cost of the improvements rather than use government funds. The project included renovating all of the rooms on the second and third floors of the White House, the press briefing room, and turning the master bedroom closet into a beauty parlor and the West Wing bedroom into a small gym. Just as Jacqueline Kennedy had done decades before, the First Lady brought White House antiques out of storage. But it was a year later, when she realized that a full china service had not been purchased since the presidency of Harry Truman, that the controversy erupted. The

Reagans enjoyed entertaining—their presidency would host 56 state dinners—but none of the White House china could accommodate a lot of guests. The First Lady ordered enough place settings for 220 people, which was almost twice as many settings as recent services that had been ordered.

Private donations were solicited to pay for the china, which cost $209,508. But with the recession continuing to dominate news headlines and American budgets, the purchase seemed extravagant and insensitive. The First Lady was accused of being out of touch. Many Americans felt that this was the wrong time to re-introduce glamor into the White House.

In some segments of the population, Reagan was perceived as a president for the rich rather than the ordinary person, a viewpoint which increased when he froze the minimum wage, cut food stamps, federal aid to local governments and the budget for public housing. Reagan's credo was that "trickle-down economics," by benefiting the rich, would eventually improve economic condition for those who were not affluent. His belief in a "trickle-down" economy was based on the theory that a successful corporate class led to prosperity for the classes below.

Reagan's Hollywood antipathy to communism remained a cornerstone of his presidency. Cuts in domestic spending were countered by increases in defense spending. He called the Soviet Union the "evil empire" and he and the staunchly conservative Prime Minister Margaret Thatcher of Great Britain were firmly allied in their opposition to the Cold War enemy. His "Reagan Doctrine" supported anti-communists in other countries, particularly in Afghanistan, which had been invaded by the Soviet Union in 1979.

Restoring America's image as a mighty superpower made Reagan's re-election almost certain. In the 1984 election, he carried every state except for Washington DC and Minnesota, which was the home state of his Democratic opponent, Vice President Walter Mondale, giving Reagan a record number of electoral votes with 525.

But not everyone was a fan. When the news broke in 1986 that the United States had sold arms to Iran in order to provide financial support for the Contra rebels fighting the Nicaraguan government, Reagan denied that he had been involved in the plot. He appointed a commission to investigate the accusations and although the commission could not find proof that he had known of the funding scheme, the commission, along with Congress, was critical of a president who could be so unaware of what was going on in his administration. Eleven members of the Reagan staff were indicted for their involvement in the Iran-Contra affair.

Although the First Lady preferred to stay in the background when political matters were on the agenda, her influence was nonetheless felt. After White House Chief of Staff Donald Regan was replaced, Regan, who believed that the First Lady had been responsible for the staffing change, revealed that Nancy Reagan consulted astrologers and used the predictions to direct Reagan's presidential schedule. Some also believed that it was Mrs. Reagan who was the one who saw the Reagan advisors change from hardline conservatives like Alexander Haig with moderates like George Schultz. The First Lady had her critics, but she was also named one of the most admired women in the United States in the annual *Good Housekeeping* and Annual Gallup Poll for each of the years that she and Ronald Reagan were in the White House.

As president, Reagan expected to be criticized, but he was also lauded for some of his victories. One of his greatest achievements as president was likely the arms reduction treaties between the United States and the Soviet Union. Working with Soviet Leader Mikhail Gorbachev, who had initiated a policy called glasnost to allow Soviet citizens to enjoy more political freedom, Reagan was able to reduce the ominous threat of nuclear war between the two nations.

He achieved equally dramatic success on the judicial front. Before Reagan, the Supreme Court was an all-male enclave. That ended in 1981 when he nominated Sandra Day O'Connor to the august judicial body. O'Connor was unanimously confirmed by the Senate, an accord which was not present six years later when Reagan's nomination of Robert Bork to the Supreme Court was vehemently rejected.

He left office in 1989 with a a presidential stature that made him a legend to the conservatives in the country. But in 1994, he announced that he was suffering from Alzheimer's disease. Even at that moment of personal disclosure, his words offered hope, as he wrote, "I now begin the journey that will lead me into the sunset of my life. I know that for America there will always be a bright dawn ahead." Reagan died ten years after announcing that he was suffering from Alzheimer's; throughout the progression of the disease, Nancy Reagan continued to care for him.

Attendees at his funeral included his British ally, former Prime Minister Margaret Thatcher, and his former Cold War foe Mikhail Gorbachev, and world leaders from Italy, Germany, Afghanistan, and Iraq. The world was a very different place from what it had been when he left office and historians will long debate whether those changes benefitted or harmed the American nation, but no one can deny that Ronald Reagan left a lasting imprint on the America he loved.

Why was Reagan Important?

Ronald Reagan is regarded as a transformational president. Regarding his triumph over the Soviet Union, British Prime Minister Margaret Thatcher described his accomplishments as a victory of his creed. Reagan, she wrote, "had achieved the most difficult of all political tasks: changing attitudes and perceptions about what is possible. From the strong fortress of his convictions, he set out to enlarge freedom the world over at a time when freedom was in retreat—and he succeeded."

Historians give his presidency mixed grades. His role in the dissolution of the Soviet Union and the end of the Cold War is not disputed, although many argue that there were other factors: Soviet defeat in Afghanistan; the breakdown of the Soviet economy following the

143

failure of Soviet economic policies; the growing desire for independence in Poland. The economic growth that resulted from his tax cuts was not supported by an increase in revenue that he'd expected.

Reagan's effect on American politics has transformed both Republican and Democrats. Bill Clinton was not elected as a liberal, but as a centrist; the Republican Party has moved further to the right, and Democrats no longer lean as far left as in pre-Reagan years. But Reagan was not an ideologue who could not work with Democrats. He worked with both his own and the opposition party on legislation for Social Security and his tax overhaul. After 40 years of Democrats dominating Congress, the Republicans won the House of Representatives in 1994, a legacy of Reagan's influence over changing voter priorities. The two-term Republican president is invoked by both parties during campaign season.

So powerful is the legend of Reagan that his presidency has already taken on mythic proportions. In 2011, upon the 100th anniversary of his birth, the *Washington Post* listed popular myths about Ronald Reagan. It's believed that he was one of America's most popular presidents, but his average approval rating during his two terms was 52.8 percent, behind

Kennedy, Clinton, Eisenhower, Lyndon Johnson, and George H.W. Bush. His popularity ratings began to ascend after the nation learned that he had Alzheimer's disease, and after the Ronald Reagan Legacy Project was successful in renaming the Washington D.C. airport for him. His reputation as a president who cut taxes ignores the fact that, except for the first and last years in office, he raised taxes. Reagan supported small government. He was famed for announcing at his first inauguration that government was not the solution to the country's existing problems, but was in fact the problem. Yet federal spending increased by 2.5 percent each year of his presidency. The national debt increased from $700 billion to almost $3 trillion. The number of federal employees increased from 2.8 million to 3 million and it was Democrat Bill Clinton who reduced federal employee numbers down to 2.7 million. Instead of reducing the number of Cabinet agencies, Reagan added the Veterans Affairs to the list.

He preached traditional values and his words found fertile ground in Americans who believed that the American ideals they treasured were valid. The inscription at Reagan's burial site in Simi Valley, California, reads "I know in my heart that man is good, that what is right will always eventually triumph and that there is purpose and worth to each and every life." Those are idealistic words from a man who was at heart, a pragmatist. He believed in the goodness of America and in post-Watergate America, the people needed to believe in themselves and their country again. Reagan's economic policies may not have brought the sustainable prosperity that he intended, but his role in the end of the Cold War brought a different kind of prosperity to the nation. With the collapse of the Soviet Union after Reagan's relentless and determined strategy to diminish the communist nation's sphere of influence, the United States found itself the only superpower. Reagan's role in that fact, along with the part he played in the rise of the conservative movement in American politics, has had a lasting effect on the nation.

Made in the USA
Lexington, KY
20 December 2018